THE COMPLETE BLOCK BOOK

THE
COMPLETE BLOCK BOOK

EUGENE F. PROVENZO, JR., & ARLENE BRETT

PHOTOGRAPHS BY MICHAEL CARLEBACH

SYRACUSE UNIVERSITY PRESS

Copyright © 1983 by SYRACUSE UNIVERSITY PRESS
Syracuse, New York 13244-5160

First Edition 1983
92 93 94 95 96 97 98   7 6 5 4 3

Library of Congress Cataloging in Publication Data

Provenzo, Eugene F.
   The complete block book.

   1. Block Building (Education)   I. Brett, Arlene.
II. Title.
LB1139.C7P76   1983   372.13′078   83-18093
ISBN 0-8156-2300-3
ISBN 0-8156-0188-3 (pbk.)

Manufactured in the United States of America

CONTENTS

ACKNOWLEDGMENTS   vii

1. **BLOCKS:** AN INTRODUCTION   1

2. **BLOCK BUILDING:** HISTORICAL SURVEY   7

3. **BLOCKS:** THEORY AND RESEARCH   35

4. **CURRENT BLOCK SYSTEMS**   63

5. **USING BLOCKS IN CLASSROOM AND HOME**   81

NOTES   105

APPENDIX A

THE ART OF BLOCK BUILDING   111
    Harriet M. Johnson

APPENDIX B

GOLDEN MEAN BLOCKS   157
    Eugene F. Provenzo, Jr.

Eugene F. Provenzo, Jr., is Professor of Education, University of Miami, and coauthor of *History of Education and Culture in America*. *Arlene Brett* is Associate Professor of Elementary Education, University of Miami, and author of *Affective Education*. Together with Robin Moore, Professor of Landscape Architecture, North Carolina State University, they are the authors of the forthcoming *The Complete Playground Book* (Syracuse University Press). *Michael Carlebach* is Assistant Professor in the Department of Communication, University of Miami. His photographs have appeared in national and international media and exhibitions.

ACKNOWLEDGMENTS

Our thanks go to the many people who have contributed to the writing of this book. Liz Christman-Rothlein, Antonia Potenza, and Alma David—colleagues and friends in Early Childhood Education—provided us with insights and encouragement. Special thanks to Emma D. Sheehy—friend and colleague of Patty Smith Hill. A research award from the Alumni Association of the School of Education and Allied Professions, University of Miami, assisted us in the collection of much of the historical data for this work. Further thanks go to George Gilpin, Associate Provost, University of Miami, for support for bibliographical research through the Research Initiation Fund for Computer Assisted Bibliographical Searches. Lyn MacCorkle, Sarah Sanchez, and Lesbia Varona of the Otto G. Richter Library, University of Miami, provided important help. Patricia Frost, Joann V. Frank, and Bernice Greene of the West Laboratory School were particularly helpful, as were Karen Sick, Julia Major, and Mita Chakrabortty of the Canterbury Day Care Center, University of Miami. Special thanks to Marianne O'Connell for her help with planning and shooting the photographs for this book. Thanks go to Peter A. Zorn, Jr., for doing illustrations included in the Introduction and Appendix A. Karen Hewitt of Burlington, Vermont, was generous with her knowledge of sources on the history of toys. Asterie Baker Provenzo deserves special thanks for her help throughout the research and writing of this project.

We wish to thank Bank Street College of Education for permission to reprint Harriet Johnson's *The Art of Block Building*.

Thomas I. Potts of Community Playthings, John F. Mongillo of the McGraw-Hill Book Company, and Beverly A. Oski of Milton Bradley Corporation were kind enough to provide information concerning materials produced by their companies. We thank them for their time and interest.

Finally, we wish to thank the children of both the West Laboratory School and the Canterbury Day Care Center for their help. This book is dedicated to them.

Miami, Florida   Eugene F. Provenzo, Jr.
Spring 1983   Arlene Brett

THE COMPLETE BLOCK BOOK

BLOCKS

AN INTRODUCTION

A culture reveals much of itself through the toys it gives its children. As the French essayist Roland Barthes explained in his work, *Mythologies,* "All the toys one commonly sees are essentially a microcosm of the adult world; they are all reduced copies of human objects, as if in the eyes of the public the child was, all told, nothing but a smaller man, a homunculus to whom must be supplied objects of his own size."[1] Barthes feels that toys have specific cultural messages implicit in them. They impose upon the child a structured way of viewing the world, and they anticipate the activities of adult life. The doctor's kit, the baby doll, the toy train, and automobile are simply translations of the adult world into the experience of the child.

For our purposes, a building block is a construction toy intended to educate as well as amuse both children and adults. Its size, design, and the materials it is made from are determined by its creator as well as by the function it is intended to serve.

Blocks are among the most important toys of an inventive nature available to children. They allow children to create and structure a world that is their own. According to Barthes, blocks do not present a ready-made world to the child. Instead: "The merest set of blocks, provided it is not too refined, implies a very different learning of the world: then the child does not in any way create meaningful objects, it matters little to him whether they have an adult name, the actions he performs are not those of a user, but those of a demiurge. He creates forms which walk, which roll, he creates life, not property: objects now act by themselves, they are no longer an inert and complicated material in the palm of his hand."[2]

The child's structuring of reality through block play continues into adult life. The construction worker building a building, the storekeeper filling shelves with things to sell, and the housekeeper cleaning a closet are all examples of adults handling objects and spatial relations in ways that recall block building.[3]

It is our belief that block building potentially provides one of the most valuable learning experiences available for young children. As play materials blocks work in many different ways. From the simple manipulations of the two-year-old, through their increasingly complex symbolic use by older children, blocks demonstrate a wide range of applications and uses. By playing with blocks the child learns the nature of basic materials, what things can be made to mean, what is allowed in the realm of the imagination, and what is permissible in the society of one's playmates. The lessons provided are basic to successfully entering adulthood and the responsibilities of adult life.

Blocks and block building pose many interesting questions for researchers. For example, as a young child Albert Einstein was fascinated with building blocks and picture puzzles. Was his interest in toys an important factor in his development as a mature thinker? What was the role of play in Einstein's work? Einstein himself touched upon this question when he explained that he was able to formulate the Theory of Relativity largely because he kept asking himself questions of time and space that only children ask.[4]

The actual role of a particular set of toys like blocks in the subsequent development of an individual can be seen in the case of the American architect Frank Lloyd Wright. In an illuminating section of his autobiography, Wright recalls how at the 1876 Philadelphia Centennial Exhibition his mother discovered an exhibit of Frederick Froebel's kindergarten toys or "Gifts." "After a sightseeing day, mother made a discovery . . . the Kindergarten! She had seen the 'Gifts' in the Exposition Building. The strips of colored paper, glazed and "matte," remarkably soft brilliant colors. Now came the geometric byplay of those charming checkered combinations! The structural figures to be made with the peas and globes. The smooth shapely maple with which to build, the sense of which never afterwards leaves the fingers: *form* becoming *feeling*."[5]

Upon her return from Philadelphia, Wright's mother purchased a set of the Froebelian Gifts for her children. Their use was to have a profound effect upon her son. Recounting his experience with the kindergarten materials many years later, Wright explained how: "small interior world of color and form now came within grasp of small fingers. Color and pattern, in the flat, in the round. Shapes that lay hidden behind the appearance all about. . . .Here was something for invention to seize, and use to create. These 'Gifts' came into the grey housein drab old Weymouth and made something live thathad never lived before."[6]

According to Wright, the virtue of the Froebelian materials "lay in the awakening of the child-mind to rhythmic structure in Nature—giving the child a sense of innate cause-and-effect otherwise far beyond child-comprehension. I soon became susceptible to constructive pattern *evolving in everything I saw*. I learned to 'see' this way and when I did, I did not care to draw casual incidentals of Nature. I wanted to design."[7]

The probable impact of Froebel's educational materials on Wright's work as an architect and designer has been discussed in detail by architectural historians and critics.[8] One need only to look at the structure and façades of his early buildings to realize their obvious relationship to the block building activities that were so important a part of his childhood.

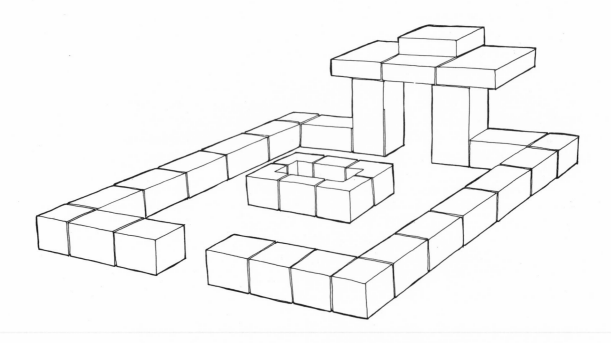

Diagram of Frank Lloyd Wright's Tokyo Imperial Palace Hotel reconstructed with Froebel's blocks in order to show the relationship between the block building activities that were an important part of his childhood and his subsequent architectural designs.

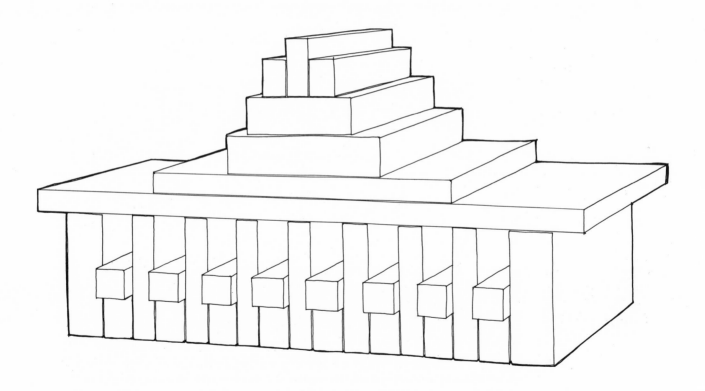

Diagram of Wright's design for Chicago's Midway Gardens using Froebel's blocks.

The following chapters describe the history, theory, design, and use of blocks, introducing the reader not only to how block systems have developed and evolved, but also how they can be used in a contemporary context. Chapter 2 examines the historical development of block designs. Chapter 3 provides an overview of the major research that has been done by psychologists and educators on the use of building blocks with children. Chapter 4 discusses currently available block systems, and Chapter 5 deals with the day to day use of blocks in early childhood settings. Two appendices—one describing the design of a totally new system of blocks invented by one of the authors, "Golden Mean Blocks"—will bring this study to its conclusion.

2

BLOCKS AND BLOCK BUILDING

HISTORICAL SURVEY

B uilding blocks encompass a wide range of materials and designs. Examples can be found made from wood, cast cement, cardboard, and plastic. Rectangular, triangular, and curved shapes are common, as are undecorated and highly ornate blocks. There are tiny building bricks typically made from stone or wood that can be held a dozen at a time in the palm of one's hand. Wooden floor blocks can measure several feet in length.

Beginnings

The origins of block building as an activity for children are obscure. It is easy to imagine a child sitting in a carpentry shop during antiquity or the Middle Ages picking up leftover scraps of wood and trying to fit them together. The earliest references to anything resembling what we would call modern building blocks come from the end of the seventeenth century. The English philosopher John Locke (1632–1704) discussed in his work *SomeThoughts on Education* a number of different educational toys. Among the most interesting was one that would eventually evolve into the modern alphabet block. As Locke described the toy and its inventor: "I know a person of great quality (more yet to be honored for his learning and virtue, than for his rank and high place), who, by pasting on the six vowels (for in our language Y is one) on the six sides of three other dice, has made this a play for his children, that he shall win, who at one cast, throws most words on these four dice."[1] Simply expanded in size and number Locke's word dice became a set of alphabet blocks.

Nineteenth century alphabet blocks.

The fact that building blocks were almost unknown prior to the beginning of the nineteenth century may well be a result of the fact that activities for children differentiated from those of adults are a relatively recent development in European history. If, as the French historian of childhood Phillipe Ariès has claimed, our modern child-centered culture did not emerge until after about 1700, then there is little reason to expect toys such as building blocks to be in widespread use before that time.[2]

The use of toys such as building blocks with children was probably encouraged by the ideas of such philosophers and educators as John Locke. The English educational theorists Maria Edgeworth and Richard Lovell Edgeworth, for example, clearly saw the potential of toys to educate, writing in the late 1790s that children "require to have things that exercise their senses of imagination, their imitative, and inventive powers."[3] Blocks provided just such a toy. With the increasing development and acceptance of educational toys such as those called for by the Edgeworths, it is not surprising to see the rapid and widespread acceptance of block building as an educational activity during the nineteenth century. In this context, the work of Frederick Froebel deserves the greatest attention.

Frontispiece from John Abbott's *The Mother at Home* (New York: American Tract Society, 1833).

Frederick Froebel

The first systematic use of children's blocks as part of an educational program was undertaken during the first half of the nineteenth century by Frederick Froebel (1782–1852). Froebel is best known as the author of the *Education of Man* (1826) and the founder of the kindergarten movement.

Froebel's educational philosophy emphasized mankind's spiritual development, but he did not overlook physical and intellectual growth. Instead Froebel saw the child's spiritual development evolving as a result of the child's ability to understand the world in which he or she lived.

Froebel's kindergarten curriculum emphasized a child's learning through play. His most original contribution was the development of what he called the "Gifts" and "Occupations," which consisted of a series of twenty educational toys and activities that were intended to provide the child with an increasing comprehension and understanding of the world.

The mystical and philosophical nature of Froebel's ideas are indicated in his Second Gift—a wooden sphere, a cube, and a cylinder. The sphere with its rounded sides was exactly the opposite of the cube with its carefully defined edges. The cylinder combined the roundness of the sphere with the precisely defined edges of the cube. Opposites were merged in a single object, or in Hegelian terms, thesis and antithesis yielded synthesis.[4]

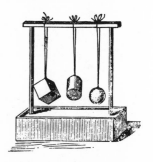

Froebel's Second Gift. From *The Addresses and Journal of Proceedings of the National Education Association*, 1876.

11

Of the educational materials developed by Froebel, the most widely used were the block systems that made up the Third through the Sixth Gifts. These were developed over an extended period from the 1820s through the 1840s. Froebel described the use of building blocks for the first time.

> The material for building in the beginning should consist of a number of wooden blocks whose base is always one inch square and whose length varies from one to twelve inches. If, then, we take twelve pieces of each length, two sets—e.g., the pieces one and eleven, the pieces two and ten inches long, etc.—will always make up a layer an inch thick and covering one foot of square surface; so that all the pieces, together with a few larger pieces, occupy a space of somewhat more than half a cubic foot. It is best to keep these in a box that has exactly these dimensions; such a box may be used in many ways in instruction, as will appear in the progress of the boy's development.

Froebel proposed that multiple sets of blocks be provided for the child so that the child could build complicated and detailed structures. Block building would force the child to "distinguish, name, and classify."[5]

The block sets that Froebel eventually developed as part of his system of Gifts and Occupations were derived from the materials described above. Froebel's system of interrelated blocks could be used either by themselves or in conjunction with one another.

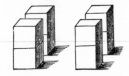

Froebel's Third Gift.

Froebel's block system worked in the following way: The Third Gift consisted of a cube divided equally down the middle, thus giving eight equal cubes. As an early description of the Gifts and Occupations explained: "the child, by this equal division, becomes acquainted with the contrast of size, and as this division satisfies the natural desire of the child to see the *inside* of things, to see *how it is made,* he begins to tread the road of rational analysis."[6] In addition, the child was able to engage in simple building activities with the blocks, as well as to begin to understand numbers.

The Fourth Gift was also a divided cube. In this case, it was split four times in order to make oblong bricks or blocks. The blocks for the Fourth Gift were twice as long as they were broad and twice as broad as they were high.

The Fifth Gift was an extension of the Third Gift, and like all of the materials in the Froebelian system represented a progression from the simple to the complex. Like the two preceding sets of blocks, the Fifth Gift consisted of a cube. This time, however, twenty-seven cubes were formed, many of which were then further subdivided into half and quarter triangular forms.

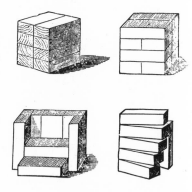

Froebel's Fourth Gift.

Froebel's Fifth Gift.

The Sixth Gift was a cube identical in size to the Fifth Gift. An extension of the Fourth Gift, it consisted of twenty-seven oblong blocks, three being divided lengthwise and six across. Combined with the Third, Fourth, and Fifth Gifts, the Sixth Gift made it possible for the child to construct a wide range of buildings and other architectural forms.[7]

By the early 1870s, widespread interest in kindergarten education had begun to develop in the United States. Increasing emphasis on teaching children technical and industrially related skills that they could eventually use in the work place made the kindergarten particularly popular among many educational reformers. With the growth of the kindergarten movement, the use of the Froebelian Gifts and Occupations, and in particular his block system, came into widespread use. Perhaps more than any other block system, Froebel's contributed to the widespread adaption and use of blocks as an important part of children's learning experiences.

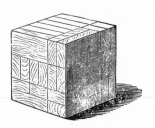

Froebel's Sixth Gift.

Photograph of the interior of the Des Peres, St. Louis, kindergarten in 1875. This kindergarten was the first successful public school kindergarten in the United States. Note the Froebel blocks on the classroom table. Courtesy of the St. Louis Public Schools.

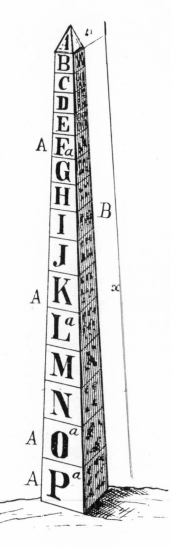

The Crandall Obelisk.

Late Nineteenth-Century Block Systems

By the beginning of the second half of the nineteenth century blocks had become one of the most popular toys available for children in both Europe and America. Numerous block systems were made from wood, cardboard, and cast stone. Many of the designs developed during this period are still in use today, including Nesting and Alphabet Blocks.

In the United States one family in particular dominated the block industry during the second half of the nineteenth century—the Crandalls. The first Crandall to manufacture toys was Benjamin Potter Crandall.

Benjamin Potter Crandall was born about 1800, and after establishing a profitable toy shop in Westerly, Rhode Island, moved to New York in 1841. Successfully setting up a new toy store, he was in business at various times with his sons Jesse Armour, Benjamin Potter, Jr., Charles Thompson, and William Edwin.

Following the Civil War, Charles T. Crandall and William Edwin Crandall continued to manufacture toys with their father, while Jesse Crandall set up his own factory. In succeeding decades, both companies manufactured some of the most interesting and original block systems ever developed.

Among the most intriguing of the systems was an interlocking set of blocks designed by Charles Crandall shortly after the Civil War. Measuring a couple of inches in length and only about a third of an inch in width, these blocks were distinguished by a comblike interlocking mechanism at each end of the block.

The Crandalls' interlocking block system became one of their most popular toys. Using the blocks, it became possible to produce extraordinary constructions. At the 1876 Philadelphia Centennial Exhibition, for example, an enormous palace was constructed using the blocks.

The Crandalls took full advantage of fads and the public's interest in the unusual. In 1880, the Egyptian obelisk known as Cleopatra's Needle was set up in New York's Central Park near the Metropolitan Museum of Art. The two-hundred ton monument had received a huge amount of publicity. The

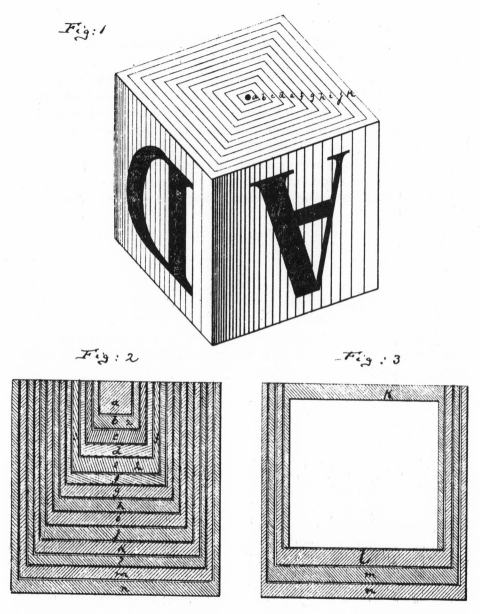

Fig: 1

Fig: 2   Fig: 3

J. A. Crandall's Nested Alphabet Blocks.

17

family quickly began to manufacture a set of building blocks based upon the obelisk. Patents were awarded to William Edwin Crandall for a "toy obelisk" in September of 1882.[8]

Among the most enduring of the Crandall block systems was Jesse Crandall's Nesting Blocks, which were patented in June of 1881.[9] Nesting blocks consisted of a series of successively smaller hollow blocks that fit one inside of the other. We do not know whether Crandall's idea was to develop a block that could be conveniently stored. But we do know that children are fascinated with them, that children use them for classifying and sorting. They remain today among the most popular block systems ever to have been developed.

The Crandall building block exhibit at the 1876 Philadelphia Centennial Exhibition. Courtesy of the Free Library of Philadelphia.

19

Although the Crandalls dominate the building-block industry during the late nineteenth century, they were not without competitors both in the United States and in Europe. Important block designs were developed in Massachusetts by individuals such as S. L. Hill and H. H. Hill during the 1860s and 1870s. A careful examination of late nineteenth-century catalogs for toy and game companies such as the McLoughlin Brothers shows many different types of alphabet and construction blocks on the market.[10]

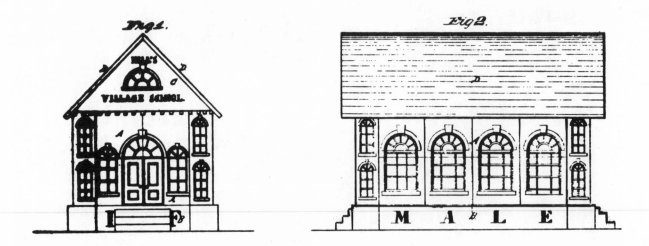

S. L. Hill's Toy Building Blocks.

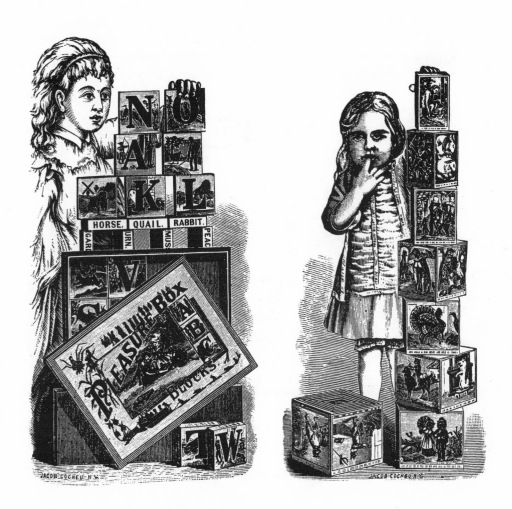

Blocks manufactured by the McLaughlin Brothers.

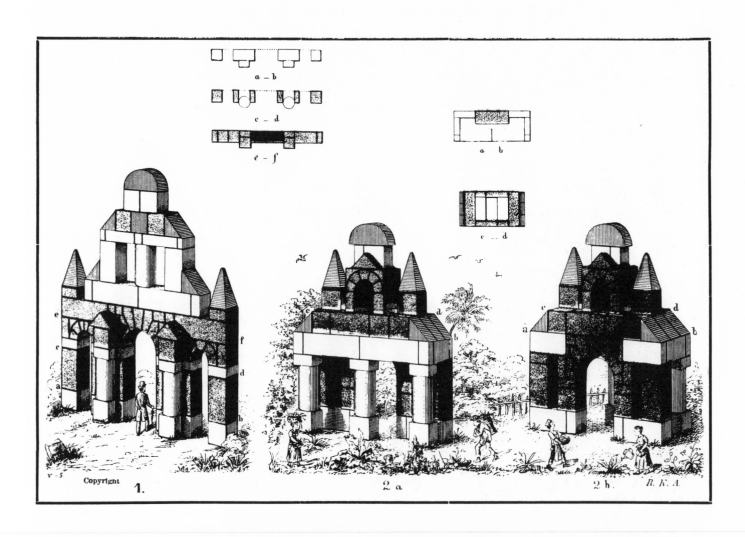

Suggested constructions for Richter Building Bricks.

Richter Building Bricks

The most popular European building blocks sold in the United States during the late nineteenth century were the Richter building bricks. Manufactured by F. D. Richter & Company of Rudolstadt, Germany, the bricks consisted of various rectangular, triangular, and round shapes cast from cement. Colored red-brick, dull blue, and grey, various sets were available for purchase. Accompanied by detailed construction plans, complicated buildings, bridges, and other structures could be made with them. A printed grid was included in most sets, helping children to set the bricks evenly when laying down the foundation of a building.[11]

Cast-stone building bricks or *Steinbaukasten* were extremely popular in Europe and America up until about the time of the First World War. In England, L. A. Lott purchased a factory that had been manufacturing Richter building bricks and began to produce building bricks under his own name. H. G. Wells commented in his book *FloorGames* (1911) on the excellence of Lott building blocks.[12]

Building Bricks illustration from H. G. Wells, *Floor Games* (1911).

23

Montessori

The use of building blocks in the teaching of young children became increasingly common during the early decades of the twentieth century. The rapid growth and development of such academic areas as psychology and child study undoubtedly contributed to the growing interest in blocks and block building. Various educational theorists began to include blocks and block play as an important part of their educational curricula for children. Among the most important of these early theorists was the Italian educator Maria Montessori (1870–1952).

Montessori was originally trained as a physician. Working with children in the Roman slums she invented a series of didactic toys whose purpose was to encourage the child's sensory, motor, and intellectual development. She objected to many of the toys that were available to children, because they were too complicated and had little to do with the real world in which they lived. As she explained: "where the manufacture of toys has been brought to such a point of complication and perfection that children have at their disposal entire dolls' houses, complete wardrobes for the dressing and undressing of dolls, kitchens where they can pretend to cook, toy animals as nearly lifelike as possible, this method seeks to give all this to the child in reality—making him an actor in a living scene."[13] Montessori felt that toys should help develop the child's inner self. Their purpose was to help the child learn to observe things, to make comparisions between objects, to form judgments and opinions, to reason and make decisions.[14]

Carefully structured block exercises were included as an important part of Montessori's curriculum for nursery-age children. The first of her block-building exercises consisted of ten wooden cubes colored pink. The sides of the cube diminished from ten centimeters to one centimeter.

Having placed the various cubes on the ground, the child was expected to set the blocks one on top of the other in descending order so as to make a tower.

Closely related to this toy was a series of ten oblong blocks twenty centimeters long with a square face on either end. These square faces

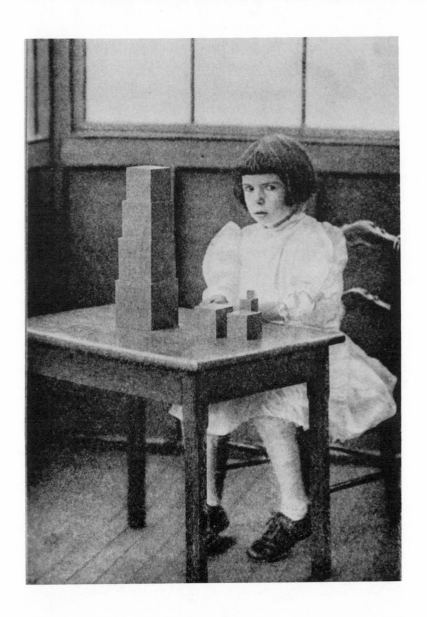

Montessori's Tower from Theodate L. Smith, *The Montessori System in Theory and Practice* (New York: Harper & Brothers Publishers, 1912).

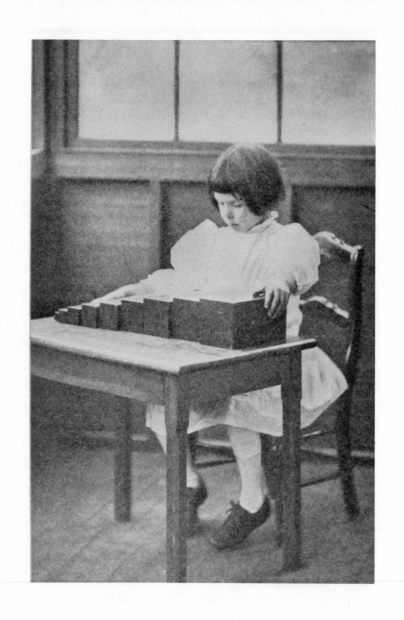

Montessori's Steps.

diminished from ten centimeters on a side to finally one centimeter on a side. As in the case of the wooden cubes, the child was supposed to scatter them on a rug and then, beginning with either the thickest or thinnest block, place them in ascending or descending order, thus forming a stair.[15]

Similar, although not strictly a block construction, were Montessori's color rods, which like her graduated oblong blocks were placed in ascending order by the child.[16]

Montessori's ideas received wide recognition during the period immediately preceding the First World War. After an initially positive reception in the United States, her methods came under increasing criticism for their supposed failure to encourage open and spontaneous activities in the child. It is interesting to note that free block play was not part of Montessori's educational program. In fact, it was not until the early 1920s that free block play was advocated for the first time as an important learning experience for children.

Caroline Pratt and the Unit Block System

After Froebel the single person most responsible for introducing block building as an activity for children into the curriculum of the schools was the American educator Caroline Pratt. Pratt was born in upstate New York in 1867. Trained in the Swedish Sloyd system of manual training, she soon became disillusioned with its woodworking and carving exercises as a means of educating young children. Beginning her work in New York City at the turn of the century, Pratt abandoned much of her prior training and began to develop her own personal philosophy of education by observing the behavior of the children she was teaching. As she explained in her work *I Learn From Children:* "A child playing on his nursery floor, constructing an entire railroad system out of blocks and odd boxes he had salvaged from the wastepaper basket, taught me that the play impulse in children is a work impulse." Pratt soon became concerned with providing children materials with which they could create a world of their own. Crayons, scissors, and

A play city built using Pratt's Unit Blocks. Frontispiece from C. Pratt's *Experimental Practice in City and Country School* (1924).

paste were obvious materials for the children to use. But what Pratt wanted was something "so flexible, so adaptable, that children could use it without guidance or control. I wanted to see them build a world; I wanted to see them re-create on their own level the life about them, in which they were too little to be participants, in which they were always spectators."[17]

Building blocks provided Pratt with a solution to her needs. While a student, Pratt had observed Patty Smith Hill's kindergarten classes at Teachers College, Columbia University. In order to provide her students with materials that they could use as part of their free play activities, Hill had developed a set of floor blocks consisting of a series of large blocks, pillars, wheels, and rods designed to give children the means by which to build objects such as houses, stores, and wagons. The blocks ranged in size from $3'' \times 3'' \times 1''$ to $36'' \times 3'' \times 1\ 1/4''$ and were made of maple. The square pillars for the system were made in two sizes, $27''$ and $15''$ high. Deep grooves were set in the side of each of the pillars into which the blocks could be slipped and held in place. A wire girder was set in holes at the top and bottom of the pillar, thus preventing the building or construction from falling.[18]

Pratt immediately saw the importance of Hill's blocks. As she explained: "Of all of the materials which I had seen offered to children ('thrust upon' would better fit the situation), these blocks of Patty Hill's seemed to me best suited to children's purposes. A simple geometrical shape could become any number of things to a child. It could be a truck or a boat or the car of a train. He could build buildings with it from barns to skyscrapers. I could see the children of my as yet unborn school constructing a complete community with blocks."[19]

Inspired by Hill, shortly before the outbreak of the First World War Pratt set up an experimental classroom as part of Hartley House—a settlement house in New York City.

Pratt worked at Hartley House for only two months, but it was here that she made her earliest set of building blocks for children. In the autumn of 1914, Pratt took over a three-room apartment at the corner of Fourth Avenue and Twelfth Street in Greenwich Village, where she established what came to be known as The City and Country School.

Patty Smith Hill's Blocks in use at Teachers College, Columbia University (c. 1930). From the collection of Dr. Alma David.

Pratt envisioned a school that had no fixed limits, no barriers. Instead it would grow and develop as did the horizons and the perspectives of the children who attended it. Block building was quickly incorporated into the school as an important part of its curriculum. Field trips to the nearby river with its docks, boats, and ships became an important part of the children's learning experiences. Playing with blocks became a means by which the children were able to recreate and expand the experiences that they had as part of their field trips: "Since the river was so rich a source of information for us, it naturally took a prominent place in the block building. The tug came into its own as the little lord of the river traffic. It towed scows, of which there were many kinds; it helped an ocean liner up the river to anchor or down the bay on an outward journey; it raced back and forth, tooting commandingly, from job to job."[20] Using blocks, entire neighborhoods were recreated by the children, ones full of commerce and activity, trade and transportation.

Pratt is best known for her invention of the Unit System of building blocks. Essentially, Pratt's Unit System consisted of a set of blocks based on a proportion of 1:2:4—half as high as they were wide, and twice as long as they were wide.

Pratt's Unit System has become the standard block system used in most nursery schools today. Detailed discussions of their use can be found in the writings of Pratt's student Harriet M. Johnson, selections of which are included in Appendix A of this book. Their simple shapes and natural proportions have made them a favorite among teachers and children. They are certainly among the finest block systems ever developed, and represent to a large extent the state of the art in building block design during the late twentieth century.

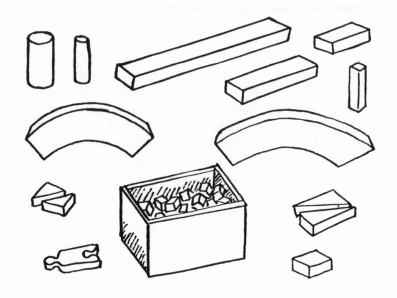

SET OF BLOCKS

Units	$1\frac{3}{8}''$ x $2\frac{3}{4}''$ x $5\frac{1}{2}''$
Half Units	$1\frac{3}{8}''$ x $2\frac{3}{4}''$ x $2\frac{3}{4}''$
Double Units	$1\frac{3}{8}''$ x $2\frac{3}{4}''$ x $11''$
Quadruple Units	$1\frac{3}{8}''$ x $2\frac{3}{4}''$ x $22''$
Pillars	$1\frac{3}{8}''$ x $1\frac{3}{8}''$ x $5\frac{1}{2}''$
Triangles	$1\frac{3}{8}''$ x $2\frac{3}{4}''$ x $2\frac{3}{4}''$
Triangles	$1\frac{3}{8}''$ x $2\frac{3}{4}''$ x $5\frac{1}{2}''$
Curves	$1\frac{3}{8}''$ x $2\frac{3}{4}''$ x about $10''$
Switches	$1\frac{3}{8}''$ x $2\frac{3}{4}''$ x about $13''$
Cylinders	$1\frac{3}{8}''$ diameter x $5\frac{1}{2}''$ long
Cylinders	$2\frac{3}{4}''$ diameter x $5\frac{1}{2}''$ long
Cubes in box	$1''$ x $1''$ x $1''$ (primary colors)

Basic shapes of Pratt's Unit Blocks. From Harriet Johnson, *The Art of Block Building* (1933).

Conclusion

The history of the development of building blocks reflects not only the history and growth of the toy industry in Europe and America, but also the development of the field of early childhood education. The wide range of block systems that have emerged in both Europe and America since the first half of the ninetheenth century demonstrates the inventiveness of various toy designers and new philosophies and methods of early childhood education.

3

BLOCKS

THEORY AND RESEARCH

P lay is an essential part of the block building experience and of the human experience in general. Various theorists have defined the importance and significance of play in different ways. According to the great Dutch historian Johan Huizinga:

> From the standpoint of form, we can define play in short as a free activity, experienced as "make-believe" and situated outside of everyday life, nevertheless capable of totally absorbing the player; an activity entirely lacking in material interest and utility. It transpires in an explicitly circumscribed time and space, as carried out in an orderly fashion according to given rules, and gives rise to group relationships which often surround themselves with mystery or emphasize through disguises their difference from the ordinary world.[1]

Erik H. Erikson, in *Childhood and Society*, describes play as allowing the individual to deal with experience by creating model situations. Play allows the individual to master reality by experimenting and planning.[2]

Erikson reminds us that Plato saw play as a means by which the individual could test the limits of the universe. For Plato, there was always an element of surprise in play, one that went beyond simply habit and repetition.[3]

Each of these theoretical models can be applied to block building. The young child playing with blocks becomes, as Huizinga suggests, totally absorbed in the make-believe world he or she creates. Oceans can be crossed in block boats. Castles and fortresses created from blocks can transform the child into a general or emperor, explorer or engineer. Blocks allow the child to use his or her imagination to make a world that is the child's own unique creation.

For Erikson, the play value of block building lies in the child's being able to construct the reality of adult life. By building a roadway of blocks, and subsequently playing with cars on the road, the child learns about the "rules of the road" and the problems of getting from one place to another. By building and furnishing a house with blocks, the child learns many things and tests social space, role models, and even life styles.

As Plato suggested, a child stacking blocks one on top of the other, in order to see how high a tower can be built, is in fact testing the limits of materials and their physical properties.

The element of surprise and discovery can be seen in a child taking two arched blocks that would normally collapse if they were leaned against one another, and placing a long flat block on top of the arches. In doing so, the child discovers that under the weight of the flat block the arched blocks will remain upright. The child has learned a basic principle of engineering and architecture, one that will allow the child to progress to the building of bridges and sophisticated arched structures.

Blocks function on many different levels as learning and educational experiences for the child. They enter into the affective, the cognitive, and the psychomotor domains of education.

Blocks and the Affective Domain

On an affective level blocks have the potential to contribute to the development of a child's self-confidence. Through mastering manipulative materials, the child is able to create a tangible product at almost any level. From the two year old creating a simple tower of blocks, to the six year old constructing an entire city, the child has a sense of accomplishment and a feeling of being in control. By changing the way a road bends or adding a new section to a building, the child can alter the entire direction and complexion of dramatic play. The changes a child makes in the blocks bring immediate and visible results. The child is in control.

Blocks stimulate imagination and creativity. The child can try an idea and see if it will come out the way the child thought it would. The flexibility and many different applications of blocks allow the child an broad range of possibilities within which to create.

On an emotional level, blocks allow the child to experiment with roles and situations perhaps not yet experienced and to work out feelings from previous experiences through dramatic play. After building a train, the child can pretend to be the engineer or the conductor. A boat made of blocks enables the child to adopt the role of a captain or an admiral of the oceans. Using a set of floor blocks, a group of children can construct an imaginary hospital setting. Recreating a hospital experience will help a child play out the stresses and fears that may have resulted from a recent hospital stay.

Shared and cooperative efforts are a natural outcome of block play. Planning and organizing an imaginary city or recreating the neighborhood in which they live as part of a block-building experience provide the child with an opportunity to plan and work together with other children. Leadership roles emerge, children take responsibilty for their share of work, and problems are resolved on a cooperative basis.

Cognitive Outcomes of Block Building

Block building involves many math and science skills, including classification, size relationships, shapes, counting, height, width, area, fractions, and ordinal and cardinal numbers. Problem solving is inherent in children's block play.

An example of the importance of block building can be seen in the development of topologiocal concepts. Blocks can introduce the child to the idea of exterior and interior, open and closed, and near and far. Building a garage and placing a car inside of it or making a fenced area in which to enclose farm animals present the child with concrete examples of how space is defined.

Another example of how blocks contribute to the cognitive development of the child can be seen in having children match blocks according to their attributes. Rectangular blocks are matched with rectangular blocks. Triangular blocks with other triangular blocks and so on. Through the activity, the child learns that different objects and things have many of the same attributes.

Reading readiness and language skills are developed and practiced in block play. In order to learn to read, children must understand that the printed letters and words are symbols for objects and actions. Blocks provide an introduction to symbolization as children use them to represent other objects. Visual discrimination, an important prereading skill, takes place as children choose which blocks to use and match them with existing structures. Language and new words emerge as children talk about what they are building and as they engage in dramatic play with the finished products of their block building. Language experience charts can be dictated by the children describing what has been built. Many aspects of stories read by the children or to them can be illustrated using block structures to confirm reading comprehension.

Through blocks the child can recreate his or her environment and clarify ideas about the world. The child can represent various aspects of community life using blocks, perhaps building a model of a place the class has

visited. Airplanes, boats, and cars illustrate different types of transportation. Through block play the child can learn first-hand about democratic principles of sharing, cooperation, leadership, and responsibility.

Blocks can help the child to develop sophisticated mapping skills by symbolically representing a room, the furniture, and its location. Mapping skills can be expanded by having children recreate their neighborhood. Drawing a simple map of what they are trying to construct can provide a useful building guide.

Special Uses of Blocks in the Cognitive Domain

Block activities are included in the two most widely used intelligence tests—the Stanford Binet and the Wechsler.[4] As part of the Stanford Binet Tests of Intelligence two year olds are asked to build a tower and a bridge out of blocks. The Wechsler Intelligence Scale for Children (WISC-R) require children to copy block designs to indicate their cognitive functioning. Other developmental and intelligence tests, such as the Denver Developmental Screening Test and the Bayley Scales of Infant Development, use block tasks to measure intelligence or developmental level.[5]

In addition to their use in the testing of children, various block-building activities have been used in recent years by special educators. Simple colored blocks have been used to teach retarded children how to recognize different colors, how to copy and sequence patterns, and how to improve their memory and counting skills.[6]

The Psychomotor Domain

Lifting, carrying, and stacking blocks provide children with obvious physical activities which help exercise the gross motor skills that are critical to normal development. Playing with various types of blocks further refines fine motor skills and eye-hand coordination. Small blocks give children an opportunity to exercise fine motor skills. Interlocking blocks and building bricks, such as Lincoln Logs and Legos, require increasingly refined and sophisticated levels of eye-hand coordination.

Blocks allow children at different stages of motor development to work cooperatively with one another. Children can work side-by-side, each creating at the level at which he or she is capable. In addition, blocks allow the child to practice an emerging skill until it is mastered.

Results of Research on Block Building

One of the earliest and most often cited research studies related to blocks and their use by children was conducted by Erik Erikson, who observed the block construction of children ages ten through twelve. He observed that the constructions of girls tended to involve rooms and enclosures. Boys created towers and other tall structures, which they often knocked down after having built them. Erikson then discussed the Freudian and pyschosexual symbolism in the block play of the children he observed. [7]

Based on Erikson's research a series of studies was undertaken during the 1970s which attempted to replicate and elaborate on his findings. Joseph Schuster found that the free choice structures of pre-adolescent boys emphasized height and thinness, while girls emphasized openings and entrances, thus confirming Erikson's findings. [8]

In a 1975 study, Pauline Clance compared the play constructions of children aged six, eleven, and sixteen and seventeen years using variables similar to those Erikson employed. Males of all ages used more blocks and included more protrusions, while females used more furniture. [9]

A 1977 study by Nancy Blackman replicated Erikson's 1941 research using thirty fourth graders and thirty sixth graders. Their block constructions were scored using the same criteria as Erikson's original study. Blackman found that sixth graders of both sexes scored higher on the feminine aspects than had the children in the 1941 study. [10]

In 1979 Allison Wilcox asked twelve year olds to build a scene from an exciting imaginary movie, using blocks and accessories. She rated structures using a revised version of Erikson's scoring system. The results generally paralleled Erikson's. [11]

Children's Choice of Block Play as an Activity

Studies of children's choices of materials and activities in the preschool have shown blocks to be a frequently chosen activity. A 1931 study by Eva Hulson and Helen Reich of the free play of four-year-old children found that blocks were chosen most often by children and used for the longest periods of time.[12]

Ruth Hartley, Lawrence Frank, and Robert Goldenson found that children chose blocks far more often than paint, clay, or other materials in the classroom. Only dramatic play approached block play in popularity.[13]

A 1961 study by E. B. Margolin and D. A. Leton investigated children's interest in block play. The children were shown pairs of pictures and asked to choose their favorite activity from each pair. A picture of block play was included in each pair. Non-block pictures were favored over those that depicted block play. The conclusion drawn from this study was that block play may not be as popular as was thought. However, the symbolic representation of blocks may not have been equivalent to the actual activity of playing with blocks. In addition, the inclusion of block play in every pair of pictures may have caused children to lose interest and select other activities in their place.[14]

A 1974 videotape study by Toshiko Ushiyama, Tomoko Shimizu, and Michiko Takahashi of the play activities of three-year-old Japanese children found that wooden blocks were not only the most popular toy among the children observed, but also the most conducive to encouraging social interaction between children.[15]

In a 1978 study by Alice Vlietstra twenty preschool children and twenty college students were given a set of picture boxes and a set of bristle blocks to play with. Both groups played with the blocks for a longer period of time than they spent with the picture boxes. The preschoolers were involved in a greater variety of activities and changed activities more often than the adults. The appeal of blocks as a manipulative type of activity was once again reconfirmed by this study.[16]

From their informal observations, teachers of young children have confirmed consistent interest in blocks. When children are allowed to choose their own activity in the preschool classroom, the block corner is always one of the most popular choices.

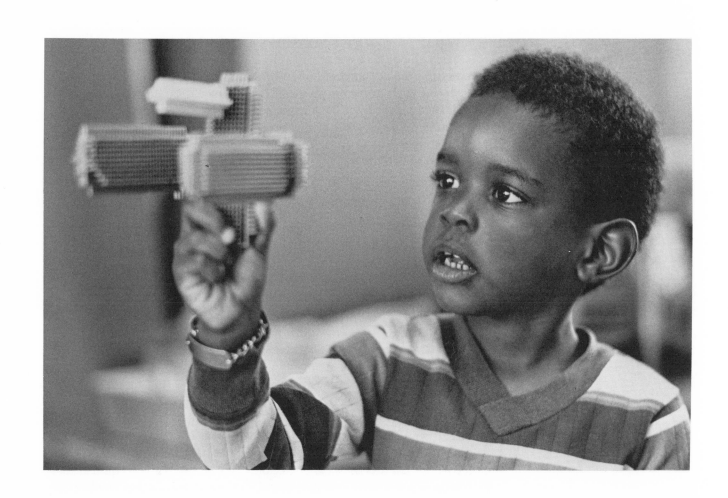

Choices of Blocks by Sex

The block area is sometimes established as "boys' territory" in early childhood classrooms, because blocks lend themselves more to what has been traditionally considered male activities. Girls are frequently physically or verbally excluded from the block play area by boys. Studies attempting to determine whether or not there is a sex-related preference in the selection of block play as an activity suggest that even with the decrease of sex-role stereotyping in our culture, blocks nonetheless seem to have a greater popularity and lasting interest among boys.

The question of sex-role stereotyping in the choice of free-play activities was investigated by Muriel Farrell in 1957. Almost four hundred children between the ages of three and seven were observed to see if there were differences between boys and girls in their choice of blocks as play materials. The study indicated that almost five times as many boys as girls played with the blocks, and that the boys played with them twice as long as the girls did.[17]

A 1977 study by Kenneth Rubin found similar results. Three-year-old boys were found to prefer block and vehicle play, while girls were observed to have a preference for art-related activities.[18]

When girls were given opportunity to play with blocks in a separate area by themselves, Margaret Varma reported in 1980 that the time which they spent playing with blocks increased dramatically.[19]

In 1969 Mary Massey observed block constructions of five-year-old boys and girls and found no difference between the complexity of the structures that they built, the time spent building them, or the number of blocks and accessories used in their construction. Clearly, when given equal access to blocks as play materials, girls were as interested and as proficient in the use of blocks as boys.[20]

Beverly Fagot observed six boys and six girls between the ages of eighteen and twenty-four months in their homes. Six observed behaviors indicated significant sex differences. Boys played with blocks and manipulated objects much more than girls. Girls played with soft toys and dolls, danced, asked for help and dressed up in adult clothes more than boys.[21]

Two studies by Betty Beeson and Ann Williams in 1979 and 1980 found that the only significant difference in the activities of a group of three-, four-, and five-year-old children at the beginning of the school year had to do with the boys' preference for block play as an activity. By the end of the year girls were using blocks as much as the boys were. The studies suggest that blocks are increasingly becoming a regular activity for both boys and girls. It is interesting to speculate that the unconscious curriculum of the preschool setting is becoming less sex stereotyped.[22]

A 1979 study by Cheryl Kinsman and Laure Berk found no indication of a sex-typed attraction to the block area. Boys and girls spent equal time playing with blocks, prefering block play to any other activity.[23]

Earlier studies found that block play was considered a boy's activity. Boys tended to dominate the use of the blocks, although girls, when given an opportunity to work with blocks, were equally interested and capable. The recent emphasis on the equalization of sex roles and the decrease in sex-role stereotyping seem to have given girls greater access to blocks as a play activity. However, there still appear to be strong parental expectations about suitable activities for boys and for girls. These expectations are often brought to the early childhood classroom by the children.

Choice of Blocks by Shape and Color

In a study by A. Granza and P. Witt to determine color preference in blocks, four and five year olds were presented with blocks of four different colors. No clear color preference emerged. Instead, the children used the blocks that were closest to them regardless of their color. The color of the blocks was evidently not significant.[24]

Shape as an important factor in children's block-building activities was explored in two studies—one by Eva Hulson and Helen Reich in 1931 and one by Kenneth Moyer and B. von Haller Gilner in 1956. In both studies, children ages three through five preferred flat rectangular blocks to blocks of other shapes.[25]

Studies on Reinforcement and Creativity with Blocks

Fifth- and sixth-grade children were given blocks and instructed to make whatever they wanted. Four different schedules of social reinforcement were employed with four different groups of children. The reinforcement had varying effects on the complexity of structures and the number of blocks used. The results of this study by Keith Barton in 1979 suggest that social reinforcement may not be effective for all people.[26]

Elizabeth Goetz and Donald Baer studied the effect of a teacher's social reinforcement on the diversity of block-building forms of three- and four-year-old girls. The girls were given praise and approval by the teacher each time a new form appeared in their constructions. The number of new forms created increased under this reinforcement. The method was changed so that the teacher reinforced the production of forms that were the same as the child had already made. The number of new forms decreased. Reinforcement modified the diveristy of block structures created by the children in this study.

In a 1977 study Kathy Chambers attempted to measure the effect of immediate reinforcement on creativity in the block construction of six to

eight year olds. Children in an experimental group were given a positive response every time they produced a new form. Children in the control group were observed without comment. The block structures of the experimental group had significantly higher form diversity scores than the control group.[28]

In a 1981 study of nine preschool children, Elizabeth Goetz noted that reinforcement again increased the number of new forms built.[29]

56

Developmental Stages in Block Building

Research attempting to determine different developmental stages in children's block construction reveals wide variations in block-building skills at different ages, but certain clear and identifiable trends in block-building emerge as children progress in age.

Attempts to use block-building activities as the basis for a developmental scale date back to the 1930s. In 1933 Marjory Bailey tried to develop a set of scales for evaluating block construction that could be used to assess children's manipulative ability. More then one hundred observers independently rated photographs of the constructions of children ages two through six. The study initially assumed that increased complexity in the constructions made by children would correlate with their age. This was not in fact the case, and further development of the scales was abandoned.[30]

In 1958 a study by Eleanor Robinson of children ages three through ten found that younger children tended to construct stacks of blocks and make serial arrangements. Enclosures appeared early in children's constructions and continued to be an important part of their structures as the children grew older. Roofed buildings followed the development of closed constructions and began in most cases around the age of five. Older children built more symmetrical and balanced buildings. As the children got older, the quality of their constructions also improved. Verbal analysis revealed that children used blocks to represent an increasing range of ideas. Younger children built simple structures, while older children made much more detailed constructions. Older children also described what they had built in greater detail and often would place their creations in an historical or geographical context.[31]

A study by Robert Schirrmacher in 1975 sought to determine whether adult modeling would affect the developmental level of block construction of preschool children. Children who experienced modeling did not build at higher levels than the control groups. Time and methodological limitations of this study were reported, and suggest the questionable values of the results.[32]

A study by Kenneth Moyer and B. von Haller Gilner in 1956 of seventy-five children, ages two through five, found strong differences in block-building ability based upon age. Older children were able to integrate blocks into more complex organizations. At all ages, girls outperformed boys. Children who previously had been rated as having superior mental abilities also performed better with block-building tasks.[33]

Stuart Reifel asked two groups of children, the first consisting of four year olds and the second of seven year olds, to use blocks to represent a story. Older children's structures were more relevant to the story and included greater detail.[34]

Miscellaneous Studies

In a 1970 study concerning children's interest and desire for enclosed play areas, A. Granza placed enterable boxes with various degrees of openness in a classroom with four year olds. During free play children showed striking preferences for the boxes with the greatest amount of enclosure.[35]

In a 1978 study Judith Bender observed and recorded the behavior of four-year-old boys playing with large building blocks. The boys were first given twenty large blocks to play with. During later sessions fifty blocks were added, making a total of seventy blocks. Bender compared observations of the boys' play behavior with different numbers of blocks and found that when the number of blocks increased, more children became involved in the building process and the subsequent play. Incidents of positive behavior greatly increased with the larger number of blocks. These positive behaviors included peer cooperation to achieve goals, disputes being settled without the teacher, structures being developed to attain privacy, structures being used as vehicles for dramatic play, and the use of related materials to extend ideas.[36]

Conclusion

Psychologists and educators have developed a significant body of research concerning the role of block-building activities in the development of children. Issues such as the psychosexual implications of block structures, the importance of block building in the psychomotor development of the child, and the role of blocks in the development of the child's creativity have only begun to be explored.

There is a need at this time for systematic research that addresses the question of how block-construction activities interrelate with other areas of cognitive development. For example, to what extent do experiences with blocks contribute to children's mathematical understanding? Does playing with blocks at a young age help them grasp concepts such as seriation and numeration more readily? Do systems closely related to children's block building activities such as the Cuisenaire rods contribute significantly to the mathematical development of the child? Does a significant relationship exist between the symbolic representation of physical structures when children play with blocks and their later acquisition of architectural and mapping skills? Do activities like block building play a critical role in the development of architectural insight and creativity, as seems to have been the case with Frank Lloyd Wright?

Further research may provide us with a more definite understanding of when children should begin playing with blocks and what are the best types of activities for them from a developmental point of view. Related to these issues is the question of which age groups most benefit from playing with blocks. The restriction of block play to early childhood is probably a serious error. Once they overcome their prejudice that playing with blocks is "for babies," elementary school children find block play both stimulating and rewarding. Why is it that an elementary school child considers it acceptable to play with Legos but not floor blocks? The perception of what is or is not a socially acceptable play activity is the source of this attitude.

Similarly, the almost total exclusion of block-building activities from the world of adolescents, young adults, and adults means that we are ig-

noring a potentially important opportunity to give people the chance to work in structuring three-dimensional forms.

In conclusion, blocks have an enormous potential to educate and entertain. In using them, parents and teachers need to be aware of their role in the affective, cognitive, and psychomotor domains. Finally, further research needs to be undertaken that will extend our understanding of the possibilities and limitations of blocks as educational toys.

4

CURRENT BLOCK SYSTEMS

Parents and teachers interested in using blocks with their children have a wide variety of choices open to them. Simple unit blocks, alphabet blocks, and interlocking systems are among the many types of building blocks currently available. It is beyond the scope of this work to argue for or against individual block systems. The suitability of a particular set of blocks will be determined by the age, developmental level, and interest of the child. Our purpose in this chapter is to provide a catalog of some of the most commonly available types of blocks and to suggest how they can be used.

Unit Blocks

Undoubtedly the most widely used system of blocks currently available are the Caroline Pratt Unit Blocks. Made from kiln-dried maple and birch, a set of Unit Blocks is one of the most durable and lasting types of toys. A well-made set of Unit Blocks has bevelled edges and has been carefully sanded. Lightly waxing the blocks when they are first purchased will provide them with a protective finish and help preserve them over the years.

The principal manufacturer of Unit Blocks in America is Childcraft Education Corporation. Childcraft sells Unit Blocks in sets of varying sizes. Childcraft's basic Kindergarten Primary Set includes twenty-seven basic shapes that are multiples or divisions of the basic unit shape which measures 1 3/8" × 2 3/4" × 5 1/2". A total of 668 blocks are included in their Comprehensive Kindergarten Primary Set. Different shapes types of sets are available.

The Unit Blocks manufactured by Childcraft are intended to be used on the floor. A smaller set of Unit Table Blocks manufactured by Childcraft is also available. The Unit Table Blocks are best used when children have to play at tables or when floor space is limited. The basic unit for the Unit Table Block is 2" × 4" × 1".

A number of supplementary blocks are available for use with the Unit System. These include arches, tunnels, flat boards for roofs and floors, and special shapes such as switches and cylinders that can be used in a variety of ways.

Other companies such as Playskool and Ideal manufacture variations of Unit Blocks. Both companies make a simple colored version of the Unit Blocks intended primarily for use by very young children. Brightly colored and non-toxic, these simplified Unit Blocks lend themselves particularly well to color naming and sorting activities.

Picture and Alphabet Blocks

Picture and alphabet blocks have been in use since the end of the seventeenth century. Many good systems are currently available. Most alphabet blocks are cubes that have letters painted or printed on each of their sides. The best systems have raised letters or pictures that allow the child not only to see the letter or picture but also to feel its shape. Playskool manufactures several different types of sets that include letters of the alphabet, pictures, numerals, and mathematical symbols.

Parquetry Blocks

Parquetry blocks come in many straight-edged geometric shapes such as triangles, diamonds, and squares. Brightly colored, they can be used for building, but are most suited for creating patterns and designs. They can be used free form on a table top, having the child create his or her own designs. Excellent matching exercises that encourage the development of visual perception result from using pattern cards with parquetry blocks. Parquetry blocks are available from Playskool and other manufacturers.

Large Hollow Blocks

Excellent large hollow blocks are manufactured by Community Playthings Childcraft. Made from 3/4-inch kiln-dried hardwood, they have a protective finish that permits them to be used both indoors and outdoors. Large hollow blocks allow children to build structures that they can stand and walk on, as well as ones they can enter. They help children develop large muscle strength and can be used to create settings (stores, puppet stages, forts, etc.) for dramatic play.

Superblocks

Superblocks are large plastic blocks made by Learning Products Incorporated. On the inside, they are hollow and are divided into several small compartments. Besides providing reinforcement and support for the block's exterior, these compartments provide a fascinating variety of nooks and crannies in which children can place objects. Superblocks are lighter than wooden blocks of equal size and are much more durable than cardboard blocks.

Large Cardboard Blocks

Childcraft and a number of other toy and educational companies manufacture large hollow cardboard blocks intended for floor use. The advantage of such blocks is that they are inexpensive and light. Although walk-in structures can be built with these blocks, they cannot be stood on and should not be used outdoors. Inexpensive variations of these blocks can be made by using different-sized cardboard cartons which can be painted or covered with contact paper, wall paper, or other decorative and protective materials.

Bristle Blocks

Playskool manufactures an interlocking system of plastic blocks known as Bristle Blocks. The unique feature of these blocks is that the bristles which project from their sides interlock, allowing children to stick them together in configurations that are not possible with more traditional block systems.

Legos

Lego bricks are an interlocking system of plastic building blocks invented in Denmark during the 1930s. The concept underlying the blocks is extremely simple. Studs are molded into the top of each brick and tubes are found underneath. This system of tubes and studs allows the bricks to be fitted together in many different ways. Elaborate constructions can be made with the bricks, and they can be used in a wide range of activities. Children can make constructions using patterns provided with the system or make creations of their own. Legos are excellent for introducing children to concepts such as place value, size, and comparisons. Legos come in a variety of sizes, making them suitable for use in many different settings. Despite their durability, if Legos are to be used in a classroom setting, it is important that the areas where they are used are carefully defined in order to avoid breakage and loss.

Conclusions

Going through the pages of a toy catalog will reveal many different types of blocks manufactured by various companies. In fact, however, despite the many different choices available most are simply variations of the systems outlined above. Other "manipulables" such as Lincoln Logs, Tangrams, Parquetry, and Cuisenaire Rods should also be considered. Whether buying these items or building blocks, selection and choice is ultimately a matter of personal judgment. Workmanship and cost, as well as their intended use, are important issues in selecting any system. However, no matter what type of blocks you select, they will remain among the most versatile and well used toys that you can provide for a child.

USING BLOCKS IN CLASSROOM AND HOME

In developing a program of block building for children, environmental issues are of critical importance. Whether in a classroom where many children use the blocks, or in the home where only a few children are likely to play with them, the way in which blocks are stored and the space available for play will determine how much and how well they are used.

There is no single right way to set up a play and storage area for blocks. Availability of space, age of the children using the blocks, type of blocks that are used, and accompanying materials such as toy trucks, animals, and other accessories will determine the type of storage and play area.

Creating a Play Area for Block Building

When choosing a space for block play a number of important guidelines should be kept in mind. These apply to block play both in a classroom setting and in the home.

1. There should be a large open space available so that there is plenty of room to build and extend structures.

2. The block area should be out of traffic so that structures are not accidentally knocked over. In addition, keeping blocks out of heavy areas of traffic make it possible to leave constructions up for extended periods of time.

3. In general blocks are best used on the floor. A flat carpet with as little pile as possible is ideal. Such a carpet will reduce noise, while providing a reasonably solid surface on which to build. A solid colored carpet provides the best background for block building.

4. Smaller construction blocks such as Legos or Lincoln Logs are generally best used at a table. This avoids the problem of pieces becoming lost or stepped on. When a large area is needed to construct a village or series of buildings, find space on the floor away from traffic.

5. In a classroom the play area for blocks should be kept away from those parts of the classroom used for quieter activities.

Storing Blocks

Blocks should be stored as close as possible to the place where they will be used. Many methods of storage are possible. To a large degree storage methods will be dictated by the space and resources available and the types of blocks being stored.

Ideally, blocks should be stored on low shelves. Outlines of the basic shapes for the blocks painted or drawn on the shelves will provide children with a guide to where each type of block belongs. Thus putting the blocks away becomes a matching and classification process. In addition, low shelves may provide a boundary for the block play area.

A good substitute for shelves is plastic milk boxes stacked on their sides. These are fairly inexpensive and can often be found in discount department stores.

If shelves are not practical then blocks can be stored in boxes, wagons, or cloth bags. Some blocks come in containers that can be used for storage. Such containers are particularly useful when used for systems with smaller parts such as Legos or similar types of small table blocks. With larger block systems, however, the original containers are usually inadequate.

A large wooden box provides an excellent place for storing blocks. The size depends upon the number of blocks being stored and whether or not more blocks are to be added to the set. Wheels or casters on the bottom of the box will make it easier to move back and forth.

A storage bag can be made out of heavy durable cloth or canvas. A drawstring at the top will make it easy to close and carry. A different bag should be provided for each set of blocks. Putting the blocks into different bags can provide children with important classification and sorting experience.

Large hollow blocks are often used outdoors but can be used very well indooors if there is adequate space. Large hollow blocks can be stacked against walls or in a corner. Children should be discouraged from stacking them higher than their shoulders, since blocks can be accidentally pulled down on them.

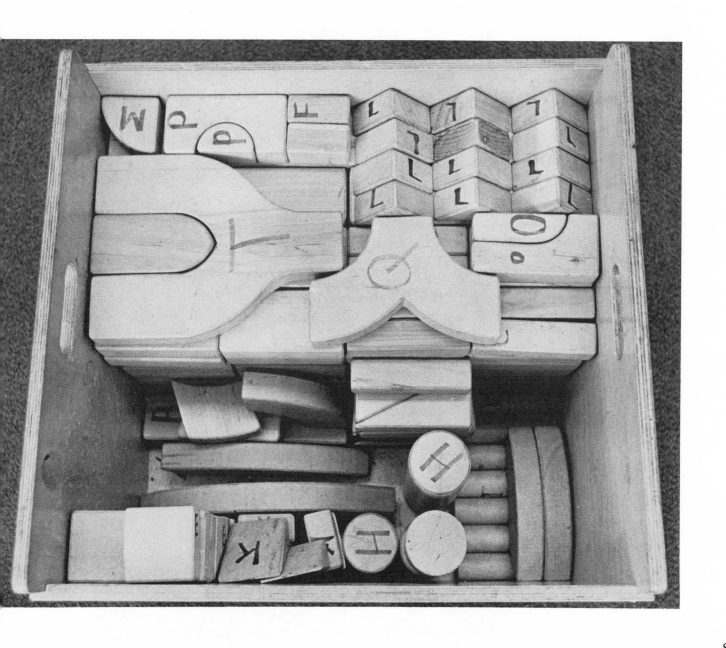

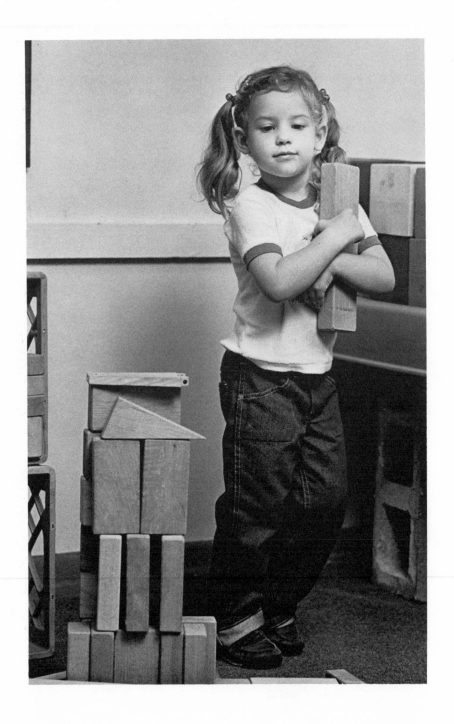

Using Blocks in the Classroom

Blocks should be part of the daily free choice activity in early childhood settings for children between the ages of two and six. Large enough segments of time need to be alloted for block-building activities, so that children can build various structures and also have enough time to use blocks for social and dramatic play.

Procedures for determining how many children can be in the block area at one time, and who those children will be, must be developed. Some teachers assign children to various centers in order to be sure that every child has experience in each area. The disadvantage of this method is that it eliminates the child's opportunity to choose the activities that he or she will take part in. Other teachers make "tickets" for each center such as color-coded circles or other shapes that are matched with the activity area or center. When a child wants to change centers the child returns the ticket for the one he or she is in and gets another for a different center. This use of tickets allows the teacher to regulate the number of children working in an area at a specific time. At the same time, this system allows children a greater degree of involvement in determining what activities they will be participate in. Another practice is to allow children to go to whatever center they wish and to work or play as long as they like.

Whatever approach is used, there should be some means of assuring equal access to all of the areas by all of the children over the course of several days. This will eliminate the problem of a popular play activity such as block building being dominated by a select group of children.

Moving blocks from the place where they are stored to where they will be used is part of the block activity. Most children gather a number of blocks so they can build without being interrupted. This hoarding of blocks

by individual children can lead to conflicts. Children sometimes resolve these conflicts with one another, but often the teacher must intervene. Similar problems can develop over building space. Children over the age of five are better able to resolve these conflicts and turn them into cooperative efforts than younger children. These conflicts rarely arise when there are adequate numbers of blocks and plenty of space to build in.

Free play is an important time for independent learning by the child. During free play the teacher should be as involved with the children as she or he is during any other part of the day. Block play requires teacher observation and supervision. Although the teacher should not direct the child's specific activities, comments and questions should stimulate and enhance the value of the block-building experience.

Blocks are an excellent means by which to encourage the development of language skills, if the teacher discusses with the children what it is they are doing. For children coming from cognitively deprived environments, block building provides a particularly rich medium in which to encourage the use of language skills. Having a child talk about what he or she has created and having the teacher ask relevant questions about what the child is doing allows the child to express ideas based upon the child's own experience. The importance of such activities not only for the development of language skills but also for for the development of self-confidence is invaluable.

Putting blocks away is an inherent part of the block experience. If the teacher gets involved, children's learning can be enhanced. Questions such as "How many blocks can you carry?" and "Where do these blocks belong?" stimulate thinking and language on the part of the child. Teacher participation also helps children organize the seemingly overwhelming task of putting the blocks away.

In kindergarten and first grade blocks can be used as part of a more structured curriculum. A set of simple desk blocks or cubes can provide each child with a concrete representation of various mathematical concepts. As in the case of Cuisinaire Rods, the creation and comparison of sets, seriation, and counting can be undertaken on an individual basis.

A Note on Block Accessories

Many different types of accessories can be effectively used with blocks. Realistic accessories such as trucks, dolls, and boats can be used to supplement various block-building activities. A fire truck might encourage a child to build a fire house, farm animals might stimulate dramatic play related to farming. Objects such as sea shells, colored stones, pieces of cardboard, or paper allow the child the opportunity to exercise his or her imagination by using these materials to represent different things. A sea shell might become a boat crossing an ocean and a piece of colored paper a bird flying through the air.

Suggested Block Building Activities

Blocks lend themsleves more to free play than to structured activities. However, despite this fact there are many ways that blocks can be used in structured settings with children by parents and teachers. The list which follows is intended to suggest some of the many ways blocks can be used creatively with children in structured learning settings.

1. Put blocks of several different shapes into a bag. Have the child close his or her eyes and pull the blocks out one at a time. With eyes still closed, have the child feel the block and tell you what shape it is (circle, square, rectangle, or triangle). If the child is unable to name the shape accurately, ask the child to describe it (round, straight edges, how many points or corners, and how many sides). After the child has described the shape, you can name it. This activity helps develop tactile sense, as well as providing practice with geometric vocabulary.

2. Trace the outline of different shaped blocks on a piece of cardboard using the blocks as patterns. Have the child place the blocks inside the traced outlines on the paper. Fine motor skills and visual discrimination are developed in this activity.

3. Sit down with a child and a set of table blocks. Take turns placing one block on top of another, trying to create the tallest tower possible. As you work together, encourage conversation, using words like "one more" and "taller than," thus encouraging vocabulary development as well as fine motor skills.

4. Take 15 or 20 blocks of various sizes, shapes, and colors and have the child sort them into piles according to some attributes (color, shape, size, etc.). Then have the child describe each group of blocks and explain why he or she placed them together.

Very young children will sort the blocks according to only one attribute, usually color. As they get older, they will take other attributes, such as shape and size, into account and will sort the blocks according to two or more attributes. Classification skills, visual discrimination, and language development are involved in this task.

5. Have a child take a group of equal sized rectangular blocks and set them up in a row so that pushing one over will initiate a domino effect with one knocking the other over. This activity requires fine-motor skills and provides for discovery of cause and effect.

6. Give children a set of blocks and have them arrange them in a series from the smallest to the largest or largest to smallest. With very young children start with only two blocks, gradually increasing the number of blocks to be ordered by the child. This is an excellent exercise, not only for visual discrimination, but also for seriation (placing things in order), which is very difficult for young children.

7. Give each child a group of blocks of different colors, shapes and sizes. Then using an identical set of blocks show the child different patterns. For example, arrange the blocks in an alternate pattern using two colors. Have the child copy the pattern with his or her own blocks.

Once the children can copy the patterns you have shown them, then make pictures of block patterns on cards that they can copy.

Next have the children extend the pattern. For example, if there are two red blocks, two green blocks, and two red blocks in a row, what should the next two blocks be?

This activity involves visual discrimination and seriation in copying a pattern and extending a pattern.

8. Make a block construction and have each child try to build one exactly like it. The complexity of the structure can vary with the developmental level of the children. Visual discrimination, fine-motor skills, and awareness of topological concepts are inherent in this activity.

9. Talk to children about the layout of a particular room or an outdoor area such as a playground. Using a set of table blocks, have them map out the room or area you are describing, thus applying topological concepts and developing simple mapping skills.

10. Take a child or group of children out into the community on a field trip to visit a farm, a local riverfront, or some similar place where adult work takes place. Have the children return to their play area and reconstruct what they saw in the community. Community awareness, mapping and topological skills, group planning, and language skills are all part of this experience.

11. Read some stories about different forms of transportation such as trains, boats, airplanes, or cars or take the children to an airport, a harbor, or a railroad station. Have them discuss their experiences. Then using large hollow blocks let them recreate their idea of a train, airplane, boat, or car. Using what they have built, encourage them to act out the roles of engineer, ship captain, airplane pilot, etc. Specialized vehicles such as ambulances and fire engines can also be built and appropriate dramatic roles acted out. Old clothes—especially hats—can particularly help the children to assume the dramatic role they are playing. Social interaction, dramatic play, language, gross motor, and topological skills are developed in this activity.

12. Talk to children about the different types of buildings found in their community (gas stations, supermarkets, churches, homes, libraries, etc.). Have them use a set of blocks to make their own

versions of these buildings, furnishing them as they see fit. The level of sophistication for this exercise will vary with the age of the children. Older children may enjoy building an entire city. Obviously the buildings and creations of older children will be more proportionally correct and include greater detail. This experience provides practice in language, fine motor, topological, and mapping skills as well as helping to develop community awareness.

13. Show the child or group of children the photograph of a well-known or particularlt interesting building. Have them build a copy of it. Take a photograph of their building and display it along with the original photograph of the building they copied. Fine motor skills, visual discrimination, topological, and mapping concepts are involved in this exercise.

14. Select a specific size block and use it as a measuring unit. Ask children to measure how many blocks high a chair is or how many blocks long a bookcase is. Have them measure each other in terms of how many blocks high they are. This could be done by having the child lie on the floor and have blocks lined up along side of him or her. Beginning concepts of units of measure as well as counting skills are provided in these measurement tasks.

15. Blocks can be used as concrete representation of mathematical concepts such as more or less and joining or separating. Each child being instructed should have a small set of blocks of the same size and shape. As the teacher or parent talks about an idea such as which is more, "5 or 7", the children can make a stack of five and make a stack of seven and compare them. In joining sets, they can put together a set of three and a set of five and count the results. Many mathematical relationships at various levels can be represented concretely using blocks.

Conclusion

The flexibility, variety, and inherently satisfying qualities of blocks make them among the finest toys available for children. The potential of blocks not only for learning, but also for enjoyment makes them an ideal vehicle of both play and education. It is our hope that the use of blocks in both formal and informal settings will increase and that a more thorough understanding of their importance will develop among teachers and parents.

NOTES

1—BLOCKS: AN INTRODUCTION

1. Roland Barthes, *Mythologies* (New York: Hill and Wang, 1972), p. 53.
2. *Ibid.,* p. 54.
3. Mary W. Moffit, "Children Learn About Science Through Block Building," in Elizabeth S. Hirsch, editor, *The Block Book* (Washington, D.C.: National Association for the Education of Young Children, 1974), p. 25.
4. Erik H. Erikson, *Toys and Reasons: Stages in the Ritualization of Experience* (New York: Norton, 1977), p. 69.
5. Frank Lloyd Wright, *An Autobiography* (New York: Modern Library, 1951), p. 13.
6. *Ibid.,* p. 14.
7. Frank Lloyd Wright, *A Testament* (New York: Brahmall House, 1957), p. 2.
8. See, for example, the discussion by Grant Carpenter Manson, *Frank Lloyd Wright to 1910* (New York: Reinhold Publishing Corporation, 1958), pp. 5–10.

2—BLOCK BUILDING: HISTORICAL SURVEY

1. John Locke, "Some Thoughts on Education," in Robert Ulich, editor, *Three Thousand Years of Educational Wisdom* (Cambridge: Harvard University Press, 1975), pp. 374–75.

2. Phillipe Ariès, *Centuries of Childhood* (New York: Vintage, 1962).

3. Maria Edgeworth and Richard Lovell Edgeworth, *Practical Education* (London: Printed for J. Johnson, 1798), Vol. 1, p.2.

4. Elizabeth Dale Ross, *The Kindergarten Crusade: The Establishment of Preschool Education in the United States* (Athens, Ohio: Ohio State University, 1976), p. 5.

5. Frederick Froebel, *The Education of Man,* translated by William Hailmann (New York: D. Appleton and Co., 1889).

6. Maria Kraus-Boelte, "Characteristics of Froebel's Method, Kindergarten Training," *Proceedings of the National Education Association* (Salem, Ohio: Allan K. Tatem Printer, 1876), p. 218.

7. *Ibid.,* p. 219.

8. Inez and Marshal McClintock, *Toys in America* (Washington: D.C., Public Affairs Press, 1961), p. 147–50.

9. J. A. Crandall, "Nested Alphabet Blocks," United States Patent No. 243,362, June 28, 1881.

10. McLoughlin Bros., *Catalogue of New Books, Games, etc.* (New York: McLoughlin Bros., no date, [c. 1890]).

11. *Designs for Architectual Models* (New York: Dr. Richter's Publishing Office, 1888).

12. Gwen White, *Antique Toys And Their Background* (New York: Arco, 1971), p. 142.

13. Maria Montessori, *Dr. Montessori's Own Handbook* (New York: Schocken, 1974), pp. 46–47.

14. *Ibid.*, p. 71.

15. *Ibid.*, p. 72.

16. William H. Kilpatrick, "Montessori and Froebel," *Kindergarten Review* 23 (April 1913): 491–96.

17. Caroline Pratt, *I Learn From Children* (New York: Cornerstone Library, 1970), pp. 17, 34.

18. Charlotte Garrison, *Permanent Play Materials for Young Children* (New York: Charles Scribner's, 1926), pp. 26–27.

19. Pratt, *I Learn from Children*, p. 35.

20. *Ibid.*, p. 47.

21. Harriet M. Johnson, *The Art of Block Building* (New York: John Day, 1933).

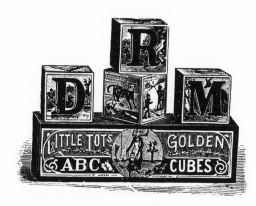

3—BLOCKS: THEORY AND RESEARCH

1. Johann Huizinga, *Homo Ludens* (Boston: Beacon Press, 1950), pp. 34–35.

2. Erik H. Erikson, *Childhood and Society,* 2nd ed. (New York: Norton, 1963), p. 195.

3. Erik H. Erikson, *Toys and Reason: Stages in the Ritualization of Experience* (New York: Norton, 1977), p. 17.

4. Lewis Terman and Maud Merrill, *Stanford-Binet Tests of Intelligence* (Boston: Houghton-Mifflin, 1973); and David Wechsler, *Preschool and Primary Scales of Intelligence* (New York: Psychological Corporation, 1963).

5. David Wechsler, *Manual for the Wechsler Intelligence Scale for Children—Revised* (New York: Psychological Corporation, 1974); William Frankenberg and Josiah Dodds, *Denver Developmental Screening Test* (Denver: Ladoca, 1970); and Nancy Bayley, *Bayley Scales of Infant Development* (New York: Psychological Corporation, 1969).

6. B. Bruno-Golden and B. Cutler, "The Development of Perception, Memory and Counting Skills: At Home or School," *The Exceptional Parent* (April 1979): 58–59.

7. Erikson, *Childhood and Society,* p. 106.

8. Joseph Schuster, "Sex Differences and Within Sex Variations in Children's Block Constructions," unpublished Doctoral Dissertation, New York University, 1973.

9. Pauline Clance, "Sex Differences in the Play Behavior of Three Age Groups," ERIC Research Report, ED1888785, 1975.

10. Nancy Blackman, "An Investigation of the Relation of Historical Change to the Sexual Identification of the Pre-Adolescent as Seen in Dramatic Block Play," unpublished Doctoral Dissertation, University of Maryland, 1977.

11. Allison Wilcox, "Sex Differences in the Play Configurations of Pre-Adolescents: A Replication and Revision," ERIC Research Report, ED177420, March 1979.

12. Eva Hulson and Helen Reich, "Blocks and the Four Year Old," *Childhood Education* 8 (October 1931): 66–68.

13. Ruth Hartley, Lawrence Frank, and Robert Goldenson, *Understanding Children's Play* (New York: Columbia University Press, 1952).

14. E. B. Margolin and D. A. Leton, "Interest of Children in Block Play," *Journal of Educational Research* 55 (September 1961): 13–18.

15. Toshiko Ushiyama, Tomoko Shimizu, and Michiko Takahashi, "Interaction Process of Two Children," *The Japanese Journal of Educational Psychology* 22 (September 1974): 176–180.

16. Alice Vlietstra, "Exploration and Play in Preschool and Adults," *Child Development* 49 (1978): 235–38.

17. Muriel Farrell, "Sex Differences in Block Play in Early Childhood," *Journal of Educational Research* 51 (December 1957): 281–84.

18. Kenneth Rubin, "The Social and Cognitive Value of Preschool Toys and Activities," *Canadian Journal of Behavioural Science* 9 (October 1977): 382–85.

19. Margaret Varma, "Sex Stereotyping and Block Play of Preschool Children," *Indian Educational Review* (July 1980): 32–37.

20. Mary Massey, "Kindergarten Children's Behavior in Block Building Situations," unpublished Doctoral Dissertation, Florida State University, 1969.

21. Beverly Fagot, "Sex Differences in Toddlers' Behavior and Parental Reaction," *Developmetal Psychology* 10 (1974): 554–58.

22. Betty Beeson and Ann Williams, "A Study of Sex Stereotyping in Child-Selected Play Activities of Preschool Children," ERIC Research Report, ED186102, November 1979; and Betty Beeson and Ann Williams, "A Follow-Up Study of Sex Stereotyping in Child Selected Play Activities of Preschool Children," ERIC Research Report, ED201390, September 1980.

23. Cheryl Kinsman and Laura Berk, "Joining the Block and Housekeeping Areas," *Young Children* 35 (November 1979): 66–75.

24. A. Gramza and P. Witt, "Choices of Colored Blocks in the Play of Preschool Children," *Perceptual and Motor Skills* 29 (1969): 783–787.

25. Hulson and Reich, "Blocks and the Four Year Old," *Childhood Education* 8 (October 1931): 66–68; and Kenneth Moyer and B. von Haller Gilner, "Experimental Study of Children's Preferences and Use of Blocks in Play," *Journal of Genetic Psychology* 89 (1956): 3–10.

26. Keith Barton, "Block Manipulation by Children as a Function of Social Reinforcement, Anxiety, Arousal and Ability Pattern," unpublished Doctoral Dissertation, George Peabody College for Teachers, 1969.

27. Elizabeth Goetz and Donald Baer, "Social Controls of Form Diversity and the Emergence of New Forms in Children's Block Building," *The Journal of Applied Behavior Analysis* 6 (1973): 209–217.

28. Kathy Chambers, Laurie Goldman, and Peter Kovesdy, "Effect of Positive Reinforcement on Creativity," *Perceptual and Motor Skills* 44 (1977): 332.

29. Elizabeth Goetz, "The Effects of Minimal Praise on the Creative Block Building of Three Year Olds," *Child Study Journal* 11 (1981): 55–67.

30. Marjory Bailey, "A Scale of Block Constructions for Young Children," *Child Development* 4 (1933): 121–139.

31. Eleanor Robinson, "The Form and Imaginative Content of Children's Block Buildings," unpublished Doctoral Dissertation, University of Minnesota, 1958.

32. Robert Schirrmacher, "Effects of Adult Modeling on the Developmental Level of Children's Block Construction Measured on an Ordinal Scale," unpublished Doctoral Dissertation, University of Illinois, 1975.

33. Moyer and Gilner, "Experimental Study of Children's Preferences and Use of Blocks in Play," *Journal of Genetic Psychology* 89 (1956): 3–10.

34. Stuart Reifel, "The Development of Symbolic Representation: The Case of Building Blocks," ERIC Research Report ED200333, April 1981.

35. A. Gramza, "Preference of Preschool Children for Enterable Play Boxes," *Perceptual and Motor Skills* 31 (1970): 177–178.

36. Judith Bender, "Large Hollow Blocks: Relationship of Quantity to Block-Building Behavior," *Young Children* 33 (September 1978): 17–23.

THE ART OF BLOCK BUILDING

Harriet M. Johnson

In the school of which I am writing,[1] and in others with which I am familiar, block building is one of the major interests. A description of the activities of these schools or a discussion of their curricula would show constructive play with blocks as a central and coordinating feature of their programs.

As I have watched block building over a period of years, the method by which children develop techniques in construction and the versatility they show in their use of blocks has been of increasing interest to me. Still more absorbing has been the realization that almost inevitably, in the block building history of group after group, there appear art forms, comparable in spirit to those produced by older children with plastic materials, such as paints or clay.

I have tried to present in these pages the use of blocks as a medium of expression and to give a glimpse of the ideas and feelings expressed by children from two to six years of age.

The first use of blocks among small children is not properly building. Blocks are carried from place to place or they may be stacked or massed in irregular, conglomerate piles before the period of construction begins. During this time a child is probably getting an experience no less real than his later one when adults can recognize the result as illustrating actual prob-

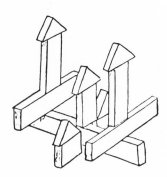

1. Nursery School of the Bureau of Educational Experiments

lems in balance, construction, design or representation. The early experience holds value because of the chance to gain acquaintance with this particular building tool by manipulation and by using various forms and various spaces.

Between two and three years of age real construction begins, and has been found to follow broadly three or four lines of development, especially as regards the techniques. Blocks in these early years are comparable to such plastic materials as crayons, paint or clay, and their use is dependent upon the impulse which is influencing the young builder. The blocks in use in the indoor playrooms are here shown.[2]

Figure 1

It will be seen that from the unit by multiplication or division all the other forms can be made, except the cylinders or curves. The cylinders conform in height to the unit and posts. The curves are of similar width and thickness. The box contains colored cubes one inch square.

It is essential that the blocks be cut very accurately so that all edges are even and that the multiples and divisions of the unit are exact, as they are tools for the children's use, and the most desirable building habits will be established only if the materials are stable and precise.

Occasionally the illustrations show other blocks than the set described above. This occurs only in the youngest groups where a wider variety of materials is provided.

The sketches of actual constructions made by the children are taken from the daily records of teachers and students. They are accurate as regards the kind and number of blocks used, but because they are made hastily and because few of us have a draftsman's ability, they are far from accurate in

2. These blocks were designed by Caroline Pratt and have always been used in the City and Country School. She has never given them her name and so they are found on the market under the name of the manufacturer and under various trade names.

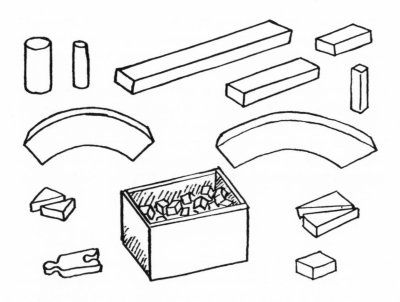

SET OF BLOCKS

Units	1⅜" x 2¾" x 5½"
Half Units	1⅜" x 2¾" x 2¾"
Double Units	1⅜" x 2¾" x 11"
Quadruple Units	1⅜" x 2¾" x 22"
Pillars	1⅜" x 1⅜" x 5½"
Triangles	1⅜" x 2¾" x 2¾"
Triangles	1⅜" x 2¾" x 5½"
Curves	1⅜" x 2¾" x about 10"
Switches	1⅜" x 2¾" x about 13"
Cylinders	1⅜" diameter x 5½" long
Cylinders	2¾" diameter x 5½" long
Cubes in box	1" x 1" x 1" (primary colors)

perspective and proportion. They are not drawn to the same scale because they were designed only as a graphic record of the day's building activity.

All parents and teachers will agree that repetition in one form or another is characteristic of the child who is just beginning to perfect his locomotion or his language. He climbs up steps only to descend and climb again. He throws a ball only to retrieve it and throw again, unless he can induce an adult to take one step in the repetitive process. After he learns to say, "I slide down" or "Want see," adults turn gray as the refrain beats on their tired ears.

It has been very interesting to us to find repetition in many forms appearing again and again as the first constructive use of blocks.

A child can repeat by piling blocks one on top of another. At first the resulting tower may be an irregular one, threatening to fall as each additional block is placed. At this stage lofty towers are not found in the records because they crash before a sketch of them can be made.

Early differences in personality traits are plainly shown here. There are children who, from the first, attempt to straighten their block edges and who do not try for perilous heights, seemingly able to judge when the last steady block is in place. There are others who fling their blocks together, not concerned with the perfection or the stability of the structure.

Whichever method individual children choose, the general tendency toward repetition is universal. Among the youngest children it almost seems as if their object was to clear all shelves, so persistently do they add another and another and another block to a tower or a row, or as will be seen, repeat a pattern over and over again.

At two years and three months Edith, who had discovered that blocks were not just luggage but building material, achieved this tower. First one block and then another, laid as nearly as possible in the same place.

Figure 2

None of the methods in use among young builders is superseded entirely by new and elaborate building techniques. Rather each form evolves into more and more detailed constructions which are more and more difficult of execution, as skill of hand and an understanding of the possibilities within the material develop.

At first the evolution takes the form of experimenting within the chosen plan. Having made a pile of blocks, perhaps all of one kind, the two-to-three-year-old varies his kind, or combines his kinds, or he does stunt building, balancing large blocks on a smaller base or on a narrow support.

Edith, two years, four months, chose the corner of the "push box" on which to build her tower. Evening of the edges became an essential technique.

Figure 3

Danny, two years, seven months, placed a tower of three cubes on each corner of his cube box. This was a task requiring care and delicacy of handling as he began on the nearer corners and reached across the first towers to place the farther ones.

Figure 4

Bobby, two years, ten months, tried repeated balancing stunts with units and half units. While placing the two top blocks he steadied those below with his left hand.

Figure 5

Henry, two years, ten months, took blocks of various sizes to make his tower. The trains and the flooring of cubes seemed to be accessories.

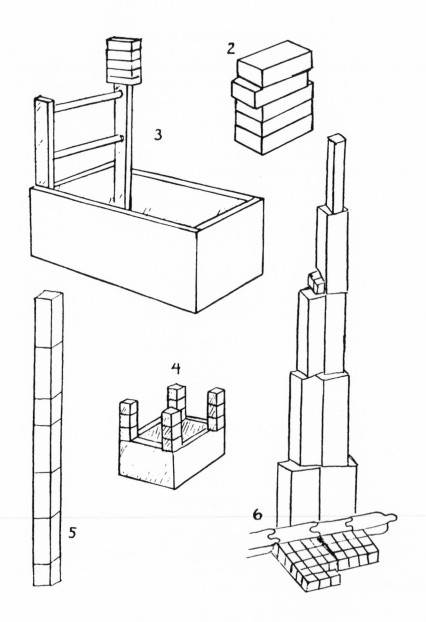

2

3

4

5

6

Figure 6

Whether or not the tower is an earlier pattern than the row it is impossible to tell with the data at hand. Traditional influences as well as modern tendencies are at work toward establishing an interest in height. Also to lay one block upon another may be a simpler process than to place one next to another in a line. The examples here given of the tower and the row were made within the same month. The recipe is similar: first one block and then another in serial order on the floor.

Later, when less hampered by the difficulties of mere manipulation of the material, children embroider the pattern in a variety of ways. Instead of laying the blocks closely side by side or edge to edge, they may space them, alternating the sizes as they place them or alternating single blocks with low tiers.

Figures 7–8–9

At two years, six months, Henry used two sizes alternately.

Figure 10

Repetition follows a syncopated rhythm in Danny's building at two years, six months.

Figure 11

At two years, nine months, Carl made quite an elaborate arrangement of half units which began as two parallel rows evenly spaced about two inches apart. He placed thirteen in one row and then in the other, as if he had missed his count.

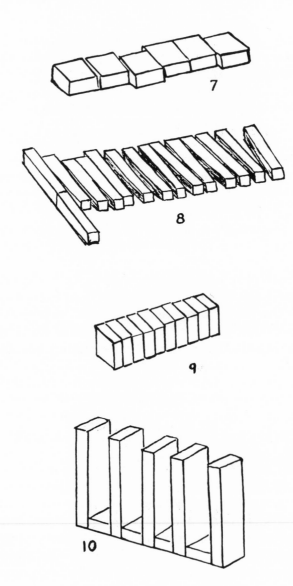

7

8

9

10

118

These two patterns, the tower and the row, are preeminently characteristic of youthful building. Sometimes towers and rows are combined as in this two year, three month effort.

Figure 12

When a child can make single towers with blocks on edge as well as flat on their faces, or with combinations of sizes or shapes, he finds that a series of towers makes a wall, just as a series of rows makes a floor.

Figures 13–14

At first, handling blocks, then arranging them in towers and rows, or walls and flooring, absorbs children. Interest in these types of construction in and of themselves is short-lived, because they are soon incorporated into more elaborate constructions. They are no longer valued as an end but only as a technique and a detail in larger architectural planning. It is almost as if the first year of building were a practice period which is to lay the foundations for the more technical work of the advanced student of four and five years!

Beneath all the examples given and illustrated runs the youthful pattern, put down one and then another and then another and then another.

After a time, given these architecturally exact building materials, certain problems in construction seem invariably to arise. By this I mean that although no patterns are set and no suggestions are made by the teachers, the constructions made increase in elaboration and in difficulty, and fairly predictable stages in the building activities can be observed.

One of the early problems is that of bridging, of setting up two blocks, leaving a space between them and roofing that space with another block.

It is sometimes a difficult problem to place the uprights at an appropriate distance apart so that the third block will bridge the space. An acute dilemma occurs when one of the longest blocks on the shelves is laid flat and

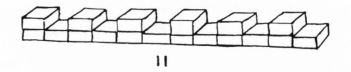

11

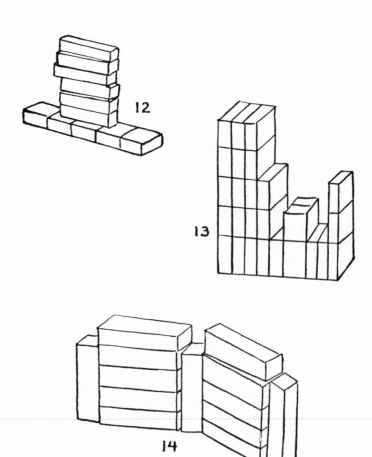

12

13

14

another is placed upright at either end of that one. Such a problem has been known completely to block a three-year-old and the younger child is usually defeated at the first failure.

Edith, two years, three months, twice set up the figure sketched, all three blocks double units, and tried to bridge the space with a double.

Figure 15

Edith, two years, four months, set up a, b, and c (doubles), and tried to bridge them as usual with another double. When she found that it would not fit, she tried it across c (dotted lines), then laid it in position x, and added y. Details of further additions unnoted.

Figure 16

Danny, two years, five months, spaced four double units on end when Henry was making a bridge unit similarly, but did no more about it.

Figure 17

Danny is here approaching success, though his bridge does not yet span a space between two uprights.

Figures 18–19

At two years, six months, he had achieved the bridge technique.

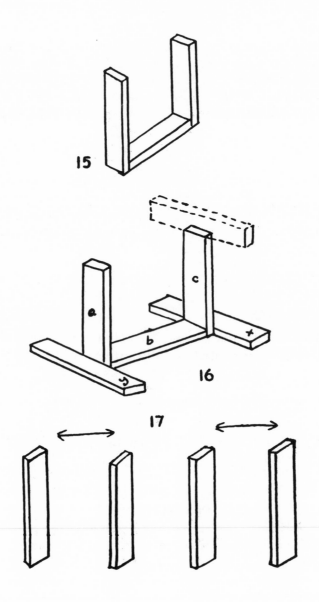

15

16

17

Figure 20

Elaboration of the bridge pattern when, at two years, seven months, he was past master in bridging. Double units a and b, and c and d, were bridged in pairs, each with a double unit on its face (m and n), which held the roofing.

Figure 21

Repetition takes possession of the young builder as soon as the new technique is established.

Figure 22

Michael, three years old, builds structures almost too complicated to sketch. There were sixteen of these arches made of posts and extending in an irregular line over a considerable surface of the floor. (Six only shown in cut).

Figure 23

Facility leads to a combination of styles and methods. The tower and the bridge form "a high building," with "fire ladders" at the side. Bobbie, two years, eleven months, built as shown then propped the three uprights against the "high building." Adults had to help him steady the building while he arranged the towers, but he managed to make the structure stand. Showed elation when the feat was accomplished, jumping and clapping his hands and smiling broadly.

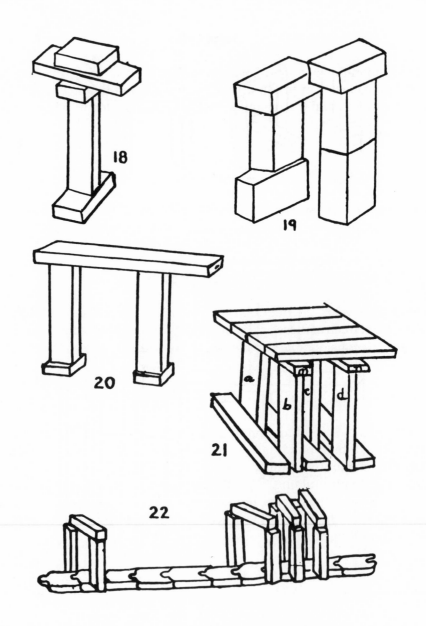

18

19

20

21

22

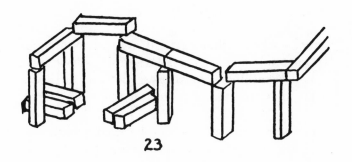

23

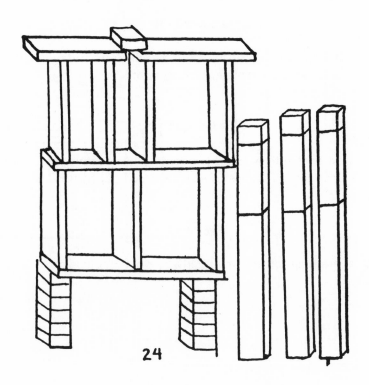

24

Figure 24

Enclosures appear early in the building activities. To put four blocks together so that a space is completely enclosed is not a simple task. It appears, however, and once learned, repetiitive enclosures seem to be the next step. That is, every new device, idea, method or pattern lends itself to the repetitive formula.

Sarah Anne, two years, three months, worked for a full month before she succeeded in placing the last block which completely enclosed a space. The driving force was her own initiative.

Figures 25–26

Sarah Anne, two years, five months, built double units and two half units as shown. A marked elaboration of her first attempt.

Figure 27

Fancy free, now that skill of hand is acquired, Sarah Anne, two years, six months, has arranged her enclosures in patterned, repetitive form.

Figure 28

Danny, two years, six months, arranged a row of four enclosures. Repetition takes the field.

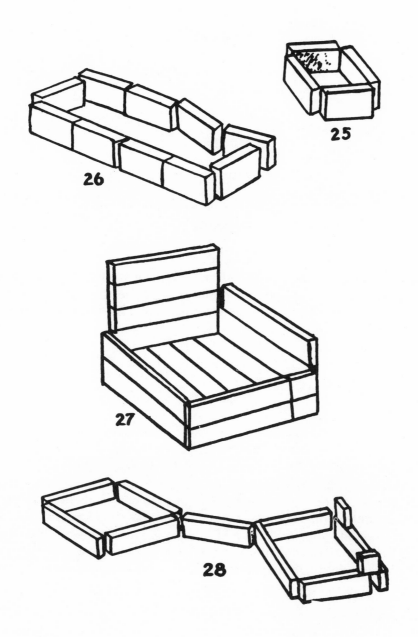

25

26

27

28

Figure 29

This time he set his enclosures on end—or are they a series of bridges? First one and then another and then another.

Figure 30

Michael, three years, one month, varies the square design.

Figure 31

Here are enclosures repeated and elaborated. Michael, three years, two months, set double units on edges, making a most pleasing pattern as shown. He began with the pentagon, then added the triangle. He did not achieve the square and triangle at the first placing of the blocks but pushed them about. Said, "Pushing them in" once as he worked. . . . Was not heard to name his building.

Figure 32

Let no academic adult here raise the question: "Do you call the child's attention to the shapes he has made, the rectangle, the triangle, the pentagon, and give him their names?" The experience which building holds for the child is varied, to be sure, but it is useless unless it springs from some impulse within him. At this stage he is wrestling with the problem of making material, which to the uninformed adult may seem factual and unyielding, take on the quality of plasticity and almost of malleability. It will yield to the child's desire. Children are absorbed, intent and satisfied during this process, as anyone who has watched a block building period can testify. Information is com-

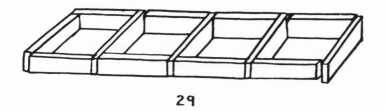

29

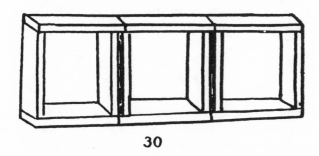

30

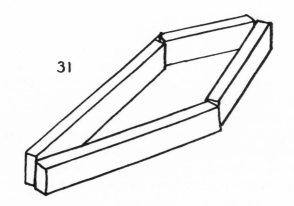

31

129

pletely irrelevant here. It would remain irrelevant even if we granted that the subject was one suited to the preschool ages.

Michael, three years, four months, still intent upon odd-shaped enclosures, builds what he calls "the wow wow circle."

Figure 33

Enclosures become elaborate at three years, ten months. This was called "a house," and dolls were placed in each section.

Figure 34

When a child is once able to see blocks as building material which is capable of being put together in an ordered arrangement, a variety of methods, patterns and techniques seem to suggest themselves to him. Between twenty-seven and thirty-one months we find examples of all the kinds of building described here, though in forms that are extremely simple and crude in execution. With age there is a steady increase in facility, imagination, elaboration of design and actual number of blocks used. If we glance back at the early appearance of the different types of building illustrated in the foregoing pages, we find that from the first trial of one building technique to the accomplishment of several kinds—from the tower through to simple bridges and enclosures—there is a very short time span.

As soon as children begin to acquire facility in the use of blocks, so that they feel at home with the material, another tendency appears, namely that of building in balanced and decorative patterns. We have been led to the conclusion that blocks are essentially the most admirable plastic material for young children, because with blocks they seem able to arrange, to design, to compose.

I do not wish to imply that any child says, even to himself, "Now I will

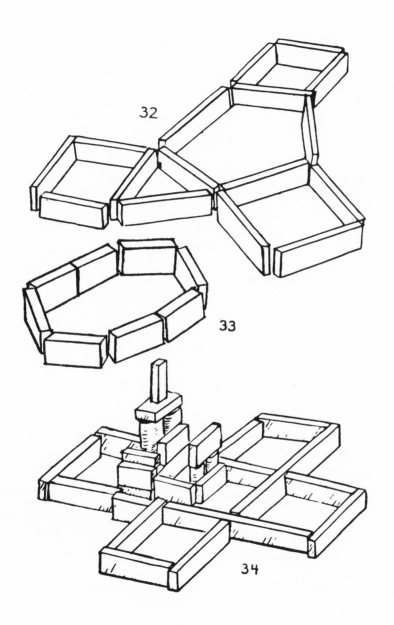

32

33

34

make a design," but that with child after child in a group, with child after child of age after age, unnamed and unused buildings appear, delightful to the adult eye in the rhythm of their balance and the originality of their design and decoration.

In such decorative buildings are incorporated any or all of the building principles described, and with them the repetitive impulse finds full scope; in fact, repetition is one of the features of design.

Again it must be said that no patterns are set the children, that no comments are made upon their buildings except in the way of general response to a given child's explanation or remark. Occasionally a child is asked, "Would you like to build?" or he is told that he may use any kind of block if he seems to be inclined to restrict himself to one size. In the beginning of the school year the children are shown the blocks and are told that they may build. The only restriction placed upon the use of the materials is that they are not to be thrown and that structures are not to be knocked down. Probably the most potent factor in establishing a creative use of blocks is the genuine interest of the teachers in block building as an expressive art—an outlet for the manifold experiences through which children are living, whether they are the intentional experiences of the school or those that life itself thrusts upon them. In children's reaction to their "work" the teachers see such evidences of interest, absorption and elation that their enthusiasm is kindled.

The patterns and techniques illustrated in the foregoing pages may not be found invariably at the ages cited, but they do occur as preliminary stages to an elaboration of the use of blocks. My point will be clearer when the later development of block building is shown.

When a child who has not had the experience with block building comes into a group at four or five years of age he seems to follow much the same order of development that younger children do, but of course passes through the various phases at a much more rapid rate of speed. Simple bridges and simple enclosures, hardly more developed than three-year-old products, are found at the early stage among four-year-olds if the materials are unfamiliar to them. The steps or stages that have been described seem invariably to appear first. The rate at which a child passes through these stages, the emphasis he places on each and the lines of development that he subsequently follows, vary with the individual.

The inclination to seek a patterned arrangement also varies, but only, I think, in degree. There are few young builders who seem to lack a feeling for pattern and balance. For the most part the design they follow is a more or less evenly balanced, almost formal one. Often the rhythm is a muscular one, that is, the child places a block at the right, then at the left, or a block at the front of a construction, then at the back. The fact that opposite sides of a large construction are in absolute balance even when the design is intricate, seems to suggest that the builder is dominated by an image, whether kinaesthetic or visual we do not know.

However, younger children, having completed structures which in the opinion of adults are quite perfect, often mass blocks all about concealing the patterns entirely in conglomerate piles, as if they either did not see the patterns or did not value them. Fours and Fives rarely do this.

Just why did Edith, at two years, four months, choose from the block shelves this varied combination? Both cubes set on top are yellow.

Figure 35

At the same age she made this very similar pattern, but here she has taken length for her accent and has placed posts—evenly spaced—on each of the double units.

Figure 36

Danny, two years, five months, still much in the stage of stacking, made this very unusual arrangement of posts. More were laid then sketched here. In spite of its being a rather tricky pattern to follow consistently, the alternation was maintained.

133

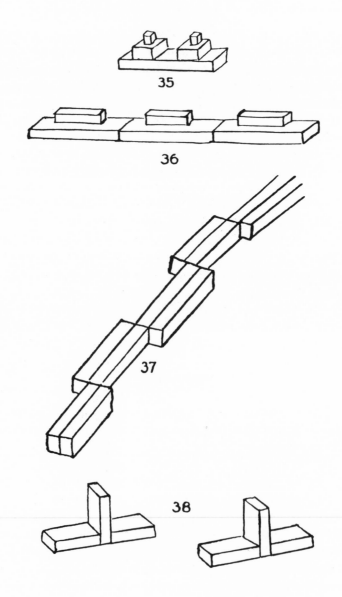

35

36

37

38

Figure 37

How can a child who has worked so little with this material, who is so immature in other details of development, in language, and indeed in block building, keep consistently in mind this sort of alternation? The answer probably is that he did not keep it in mind but in muscle, or at least that it was feeling, not thinking that guided him.

Sometimes the pattern is a small one, repeated again and again. Sarah Anne, two years, six months, used posts as illustrated.

Figure 38

We watch for a slip, but with automatic precision, having set at one side one block on its face with two on edge atop, a child "remembers" to place them in exactly the same position on the other side. This is true even when edges are not set precisely. Joan, two years, seven months, tended to build rather small, beautifully balanced units.

Figure 39

Michael, three years, made much conversation about his structure, which he named a train. Apparently he began his building with a definite alternating pattern, but was unable to carry it through consistently.

Figure 40

Michael, three years, one month, made his arrangement of cubes. At this date he also made the diamond-shaped enclosure.

Figure 41

This design in layers, small cubes tucked between rows of larger blocks, appears frequently. Tony, three years, one month, did not name his construction.

Figure 42

Tony, three years, two months. Spreading, flat buildings were characteristic of Tony. The conventional balance does not possess him as it seems to possess some children, but to the adult onlooker the design element has charm.

At this age naming may be a part of building so this is "Big, long, long train."

Figure 43

Tony, three years, six months. This building which Tony made four months later was unnamed. It illustrates the way structures become more intricate as children grow older.

Figure 44

One feels a lovely balance in Ingrid's building, made at three years, seven months. She made just this, then left it. She did not name it.

Figure 45

A month later she built this variation of the Greek Key pattern. She gave it no name.

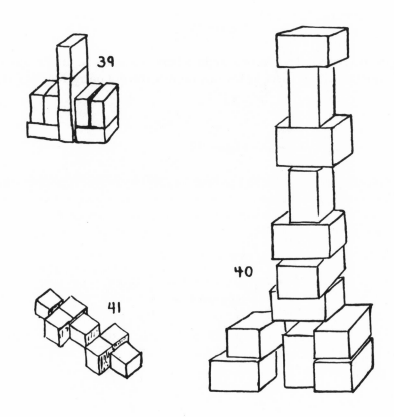

39

40

41

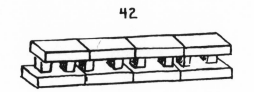

42

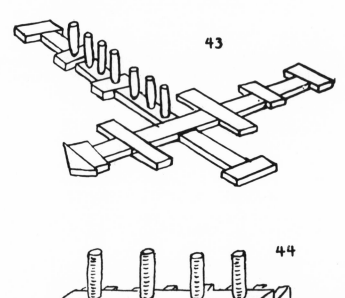

43

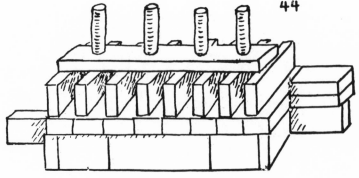

44

45

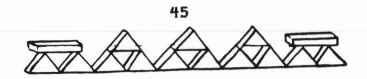

Figure 46

Betty, three years, eight months. At the right there was a higher structure which was not sketched in detail. The portion sketched was named, "This is some beds."

Figure 47

At four Judith made this turnstile arrangement. She did not give it a name.

Figure 48

Rather a difficult task this, to balance long blocks on their edges and to place the upright unit with its triangle cap at a point where it can hold the balance. Judith, four years.

Figure 49

John, four years, two months. No name recorded but "tracks" mentioned.

Figure 50

Judith, four years, three months. A child who is aware of an intention, for she called this "decoration."

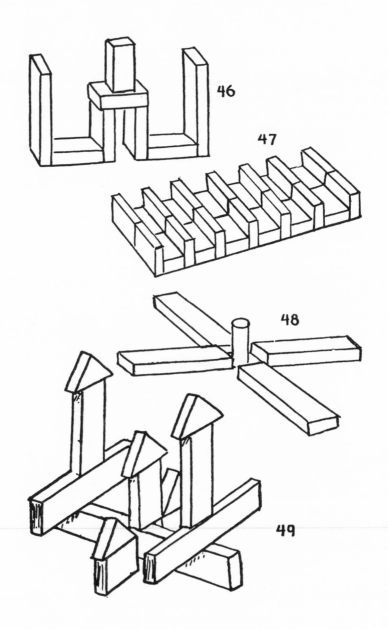

46

47

48

49

Figure 51

Somewhere along in the early block building history an impulse to name arises. This does not mean that the buildings resemble the things they are called. Children may give names to their constructions, or their drawings, because of the example of older children, who do so with intention, or, which is more probable, because of injudicious adult questioning. Teachers are quite careful to avoid suggesting, even by questions, that children name their buildings, because they have learned that real representative building comes at a later stage.

Among two- and three-year-old children we find naming but very rarely play use of the structures made with the small indoor blocks. Naming becomes very usual among older children. The name is often announced as an advance plan. Dramatic use of buildings increases at four and five. The techniques of building are well learned so that the material is no longer master of the situation as it is at two years.

At five or six the dramatic impulse is so strong that the buildings reproduce or symbolize actual structures or experiences which the children are recalling, and serve as stage settings. A group of five-year-old children built a railway system, track, stations, switching engines, a tower for the signal man, and even the building to which the railroad employees go to get their watches tested. These standpatter[3] employees took their meals on a roof garden constructed by one of the girls in the group. All the buildings in this play scheme were built by individuals, but the play with them afterward was co-operative and interrelated. Play of this sort represents a fairly mature understanding.

Other materials, like crayons and clay, are more freely in use and serve as supplements to the play or as elaborations of it. Tools have been introduced so that bench products can be made and added to the scheme of play of which the blockbuilding is the center.

3. Dolls made of copper wire, with lead feet and wooden beads for heads and hands.

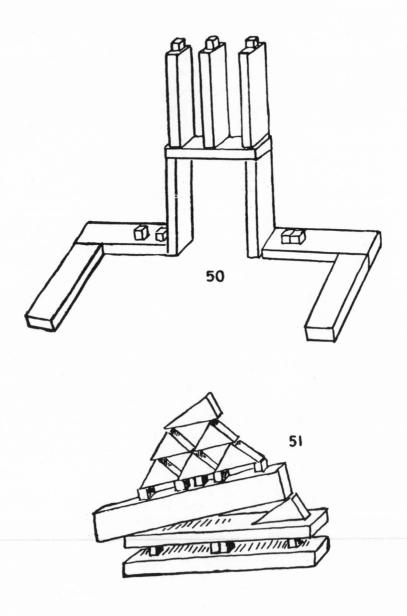

50

51

With all the opportunities for elaboration of the representative structures we find some surprising, though probably logical, developments. In the first place we realize as we look at the block buildings that repetition continues to be much in evidence. The tower has grown more complicated, but its construction still means placing first one block and then another in a pile of sorts. The pile may be foursquare, made of repeated bridge units, superimposed one upon another, or it may be an enclosure of solid walls. Children call upon all the techniques they acquired in their early experimenting period, combining the simple patterns, including many in a single structure, and using many more blocks in the process. Secondly, with the increasing tendency of children to give names to their structures, we find the design elements persisting and becoming more intricate and at the same time taking on attributes which we usually associate with symbolism as we know it in the art sense.

Henry's building, at two years, ten months, strikes a commonly accepted pattern in general movement, the larger base narrowing to the slender, terminal tower, quite in unrecognized acceptance of New York's set-back fashion. Henry's name for his tower, "a park," may have meant that he had observed buildings in a park or, more probably, it may have been an overflow from his awakening social and language interest. That he also mentioned bridges, smokestacks and doors to the entranced Joan, who listened, watched and tried to direct him, suggests that his language was not closely related to his building. The three small blocks at the tip of the tower were called "lights."

Figure 52

Andrea's "Empire State," built when she was just five, is an illustration of a very practical cob house construction with very little elaboration. Its name is almost inevitable since Manhattan is dominated by that vertiginous piece of architecture.

Figure 53

Stair-building is popular in four- and five-year building. We have found only one example of graduated steps made in the two- to three-year-old groups. These appeared in a conglomerate pile and were not used nor named nor repeated, so we concluded that it was an accidental arrangement, and that its representative significance was not recognized.

Edith, at two years, four months, and Danny, at two years, seven months, were both noted as using blocks in slanting positions a good deal. No name given.

Figure 54

Danny, two years, seven months. No name was given but trains were run over the structure with no success.

Figure 55

Tony, three years, three months. Gave building no name. At this stage all these structures seem like examples of the balanced, designed building already illustrated.

Figure 56

When a child of three years, eight months, called a scattered pile of blocks "stairs," he was asked by the teacher to build some. He then arranged blocks in this formation.

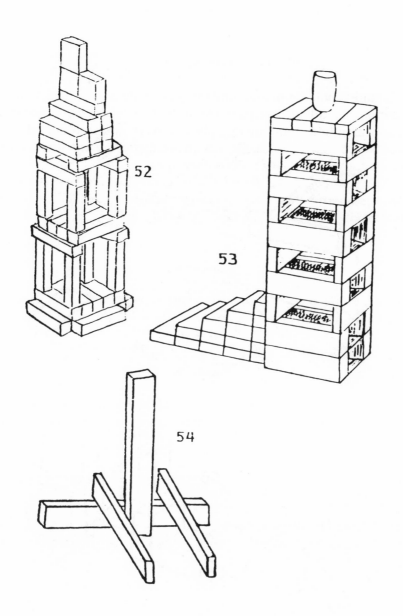

52

53

54

145

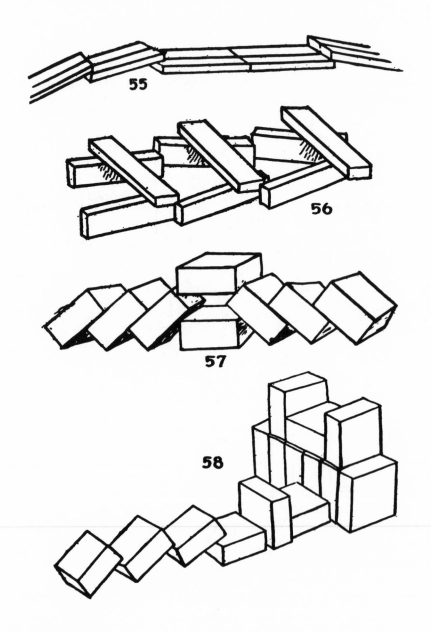

55

56

57

58

Figure 57

Finally Betty, three years, ten months, came through with a statement: "A house and these are the stairs."

Figure 58

Do little children see stairs in some such pattern or are they unable to grasp the technique of making gradually decreasing piles, set side by side? Since they can build a train shed completely enclosed, so that no train can enter or leave it, since they make a high chair for the baby taller than the house in which it is to be placed, since the early drawing of a boat may be a collection of smokestacks and funnels, we know that the young hand needs much practice and that though the young mind can assimilate certain outstanding features, it does not take in a total complicated conception.

At five, Andrea was quite capable of using stairs as part of a beautifully balanced building, and of arranging doll blankets on them as carpets.

Figure 59

The really dramatic quality about these young builders is not their mastery of techniques but their attitude toward the material. It is essentially that of the artist. Even when they do representative building it is the essence, not the bald form, that they make alive. We adults are prosaic in the use of our skills. We learn to speak or to write, and thereafter practice these arts in a strictly utilitarian and unimaginative fashion. It is a rare person whose speech is marked by originality, or whose thoughts find expression in written language that seems really his own—that has the quality of the individual producing it.

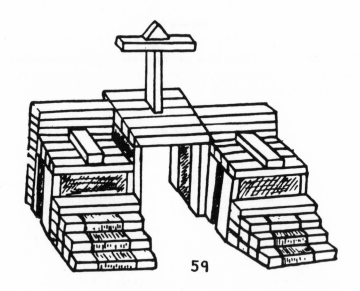

59

The child speaks with his blocks. He says in his own way what he has to say. It may be fanciful or humorous. He may express a resemblance or a parallel in his building, or a symbol may stand for a complex conception.

Jeanne, at four years, one month, sees her two cylinders as "candlesticks," and so do we.

Figure 60

"The river, that goes up and down like waves," was as effective to Jan, at four years, three months, as an inspired simile to an older poet.

Figure 61

Even at four years, seven months, one may still think of machines as children and as members of a family, so Edward makes a fleet or a litter of "baby airplanes with the mama plane."

Figure 62

Jackie's "horse with me on it" is an example of how little the limitations of his material need cramp a five-year-old.

Figure 63

Richard's "Empire State" is "like the real one, big at the bottom and then smaller and then smaller."

Figure 64

Peter's "Chrysler Building," five years, five months, has some neat architectural problems involved in its construction, and the name tag, made by the teacher at his request, is a tribute to its height, not to its detail.

Figure 65

John, four years, nine months, and Lucio, five years, two months, saw these blocks, set up on their ends, with imaginative eyes. It is "a parade,"—not quite so orderly as some. Perhaps the crowd is gathered to welcome a visiting celebrity. Even the airplanes are here.

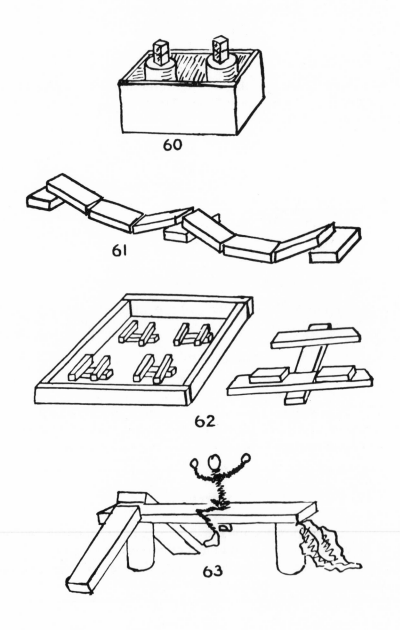

60

61

62

63

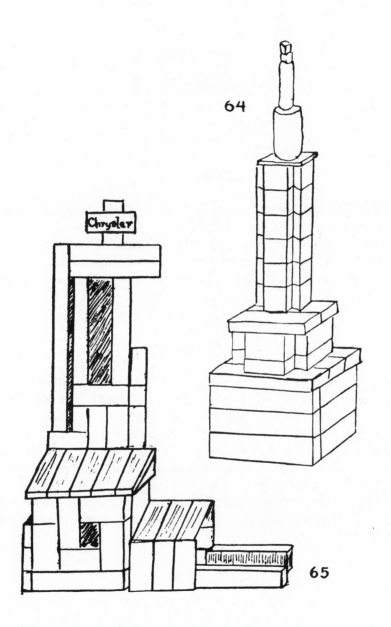

64

Chrysler

65

Figure 66

Judith four years, eleven months, has used a wide variety of material in her unnamed structure. Its balance is not entirely conventional, and therefore perhaps more pleasing to adults.

Figure 67

Norman's "hospital," in its arrangement of planes and lines, has a modern flavor startling to adults. We cannot know what it meant to him—not an experiment in planes, we may be sure, at the age of five years only, but some sort of an affective experience was his as he worked, absorbed, sober, intent, oblivious of the other builders till the last zigzag block was laid and his work was finished.

Figure 68

Joel's unnamed structure, made when she was just six, shows some outstanding features in balance. Note that she has matched the cubes in colors from the right to the left side. She has let in three windows in each of her side walls. Two of them are made after the classic design favored by four- and five-year-old builders. In these the opening will just take a half-unit block. Put in place it closes the window, as can be seen. The third window on either side has a slightly different construction, making a larger opening. She has apparently raised the sash, holding it up with an arrangement of three cubes, two red and one green. The opposite side of this structure is identical with the one sketched.

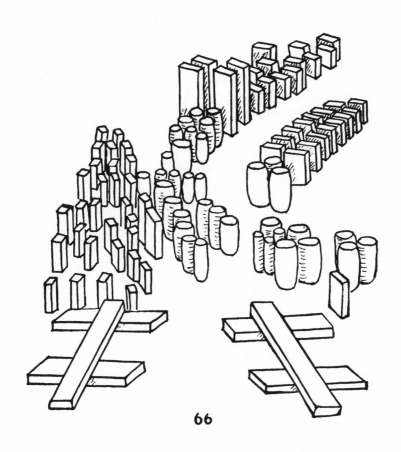

66

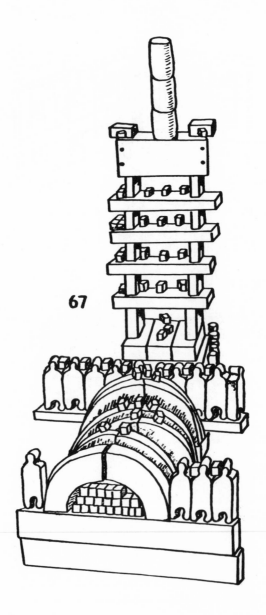

67

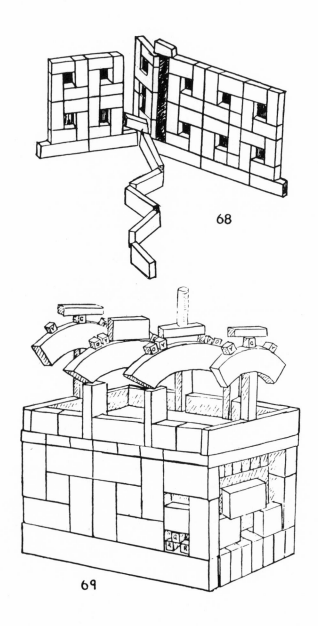

68

69

Figure 69

And so it goes.

The difficulty in gathering these examples from our records has been in deciding which among many to include. Many of the most intricate and enchanting constructions were too elaborate for the lay hand to sketch.

For the most part I have emphasized what I have called the use of blocks as art material rather than their use in dramatic reproduction—the play with form and balance in their use, rather than with representation and utility.

At about six or seven, when children are old enough to get satisfaction in their handling of paints and clay and wood, blocks seem to have served their usefulness as expressive materials.

We have not realized sufficiently the richness of this kind of play material on the one hand, nor the richness of children's imaginative resources on the other. No adult could have planned a didactic method which could have stimulated children to this sort of activity, but also no such building is found unless favorable conditions are made for it. These include a lavish supply of materials, and a program that gives to children first-hand experiences which make them more aware of the world and their place in it. Added to this is an attitude on the part of the teacher that the interest of children in construction is significant and must be protected. She will feel a genuine enthusiasm for the block building program after she has watched such development as the preceding material would indicate.

The details of the teaching techniques which help develop profitable use of blocks cannot be discussed here, but the essentials are a recognition of the possibilities in block building, actual respect for and interest in the activity, the provision of space and time for it and the protection of the children from interruption and encroachment from less interested individuals. Given such conditions and such a teacher attitude, I believe that in any group of normal children the progressive development of structures such as these will be found.

Golden Mean Blocks

Eugene F. Provenzo, Jr.

G olden Mean Blocks are a unit system of blocks. They can be fabricated in hardwoods such as maple or birch or molded from plastic. Many of the approximate shapes and sizes for the Golden Mean Blocks can be found in other block systems. Others are unique to the Golden Mean system. What unifies the system, and makes it particularly valuable in teaching children principles of structure and design, is the proportion of the Golden Mean. Unlike systems such as the Caroline Pratt blocks, which are based upon multiples of two, the Golden Mean Blocks are based upon the ratio of the Golden Mean which is .618034 to 1.0000. Such a system conforms much more closely to Nature than the symmetrical form of the Pratt blocks or the older Froebelian blocks. The Golden Mean proportion and in turn the Golden Mean Blocks are asymptotic.

The Golden Mean is a relationship found both in Nature and in man-made forms. The ratio of .618034 to 1.0000 is the basis for the shells of snails and the great spiral galaxies of outer space, as well as such man made objects as the shape of playing cards, the pyramids, and the Parthenon. The proportion of the Golden Mean is expressed in the illustration of rectangle A. This type of rectangle is known as a golden rectangle. Its width is equal to .618034 of its length. If you draw a square in one end of a golden rectangle you are left with another smaller golden rectangle as shown in rectangle B. This division can be repeated infinitely. No matter how often the golden rectangle is divided, the proportion of the square to the rest of the rectangle is always .618034 to 1.0000, as illustrated in rectangle C.

When you connect the center points of the successive squares in a golden rectangle, as illustrated in rectangle D, you draw a stiff spiral that becomes increasingly larger as it moves farther and farther from its center. Each section of the spiral is .618034 of the previous section, thus conforming to the proportion of the Golden Mean. This spiral, illustrated ideally in rectangle E, is represented by a mathematical sequence discovered by the Italian Renaissance mathematician Leonardo Fibonacci. This sequence is produced by beginning with the number 1 and adding the last two numbers to the next number: 1,1,2,3,5,8,13,21,34, . . .

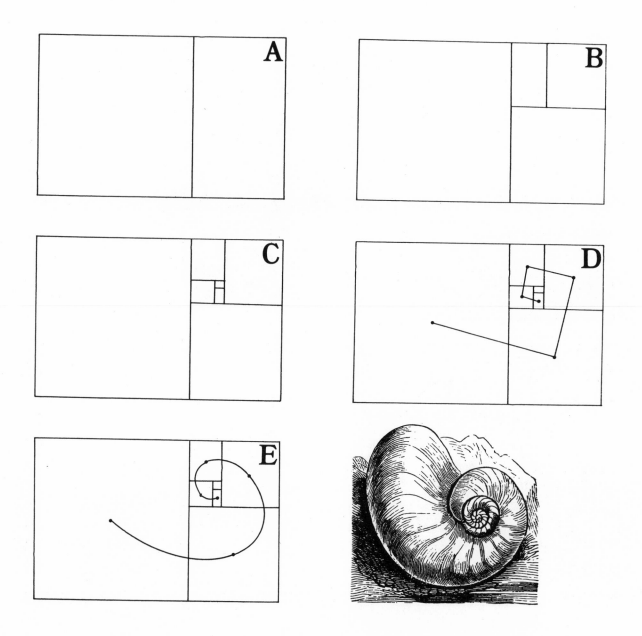

A

B

C

D

E

159

If you look around, you can find the proportion of the Fibonaccian sequence and the Golden Mean everywhere. Look at the horns of a ram, a sea shell, the shape of many windows, or picture frames.

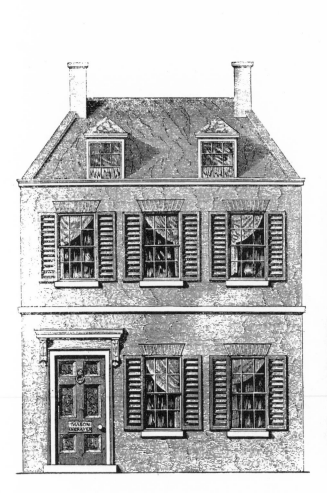

160

As Leonardo Da Vinci observed, man himself conforms to the proportion of the Golden Mean. Perhaps as a result it should not be surprising that the Golden Mean is be found in so much of man's art and architecture. In fact, Le Corbusier developed an entire system of architecture around the proportion of the Golden Mean. Le Corbusier called this system Le Modular.

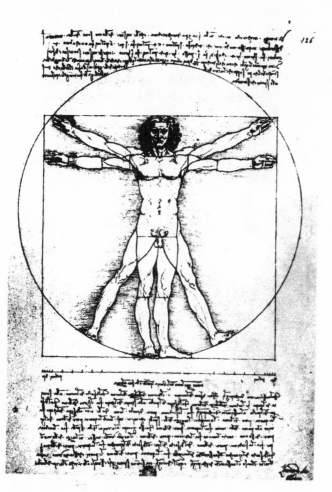

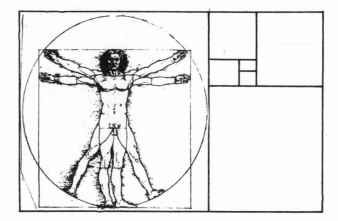

Le Corbusier developed Le Modular in the following way. He estimated the average man's height at 183 centimeters (about 6 feet). He then divided the figure according to the proportion of the Golden Mean (.618034 to 1.0000) and arrived at a measurement of 113 centimeters. Like Leonardo, Le Corbusier found that this measurement corresponds approximately to the height from the floor to the man's navel. Le Corbusier then divided his figure's navel height in the same way and continued with subdivisions until he obtained a related series of smaller and smaller measurements. He then discovered, as had Leonardo that a man's height with an upraised arm is twice the height ofthe navel—226 centimeters (about 7 feet). Using these measurements Le Corbusier developed a basic figure representing the principle of the Le Modular system.

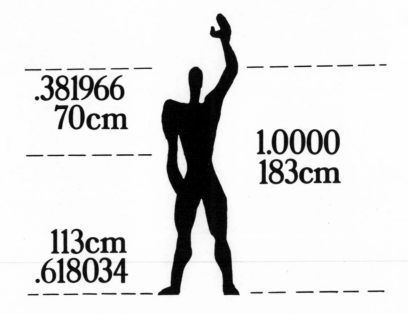

Le Corbusier incorportated the Golden Mean proportion in the designs of a great many of his buildings. In the public apartments which he designed for Marsielles, as well as the designs for such homes as a villa in the town of Garches, the Golden Mean ratio provides the basis for the proportions of the structure.

Each of the blocks included in the Golden Mean system is based upon a golden rectangle measuring 2″ × 3 3/16″. Using this golden rectangle as the

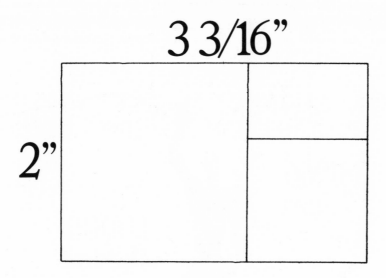

primary unit for the system the following are examples of solid blocks derived from this 2″ × 3 3/16″ golden rectangle. Blocks I-IV are related to each other according to the Fibonaccian sequence: Block I plus Block II equals Block III. Block II plus Block III equals Block IV. Theoretically, the system can be expanded infinitely by increasing the length of the blocks according to the Fibonaccian progression.

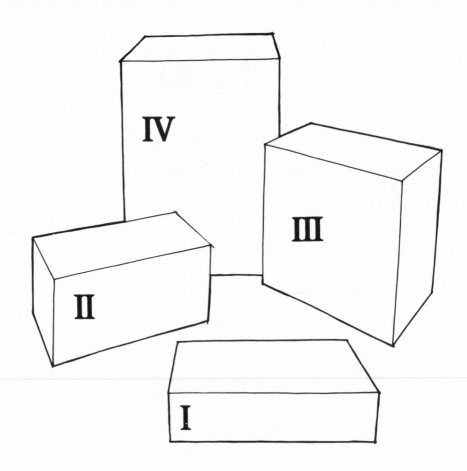

Arches and quarter pillars are derived from the basic 2″×3 3/16″ golden rectangle used throughout the system.

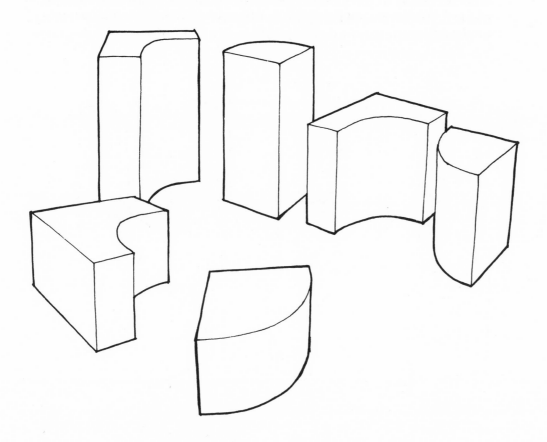

Related shapes for the system are derived by dividing each of the solid blocks (Blocks I–IV) using a golden rectangle 2″ × 3 3/16″. Rectangular, triangular, and curved blocks are each derived from this standard golden rectangle. The divisions of Blocks I–IV into rectangular and triangular forms are as follows.

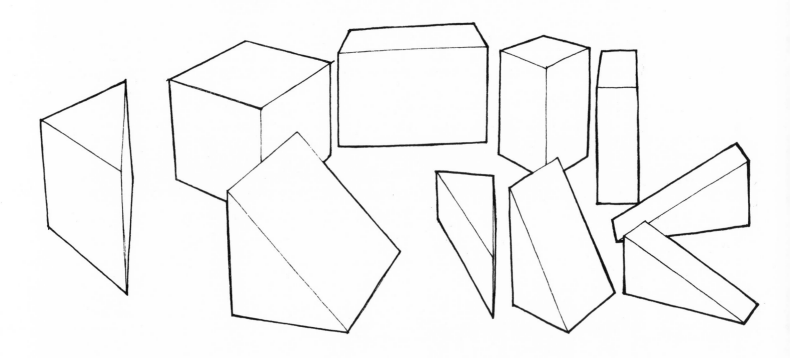

Since each block included in the system is based upon the Golden Mean ratio and is related as part of a Fibonaccian sequence not only to the standard block measuring $2'' \times 2'' \times 3\ 3/16''$, but to every other block in the system, no matter which blocks from the system are combined, the form created will be clearly interrelated and unified by the Golden Mean proportions.

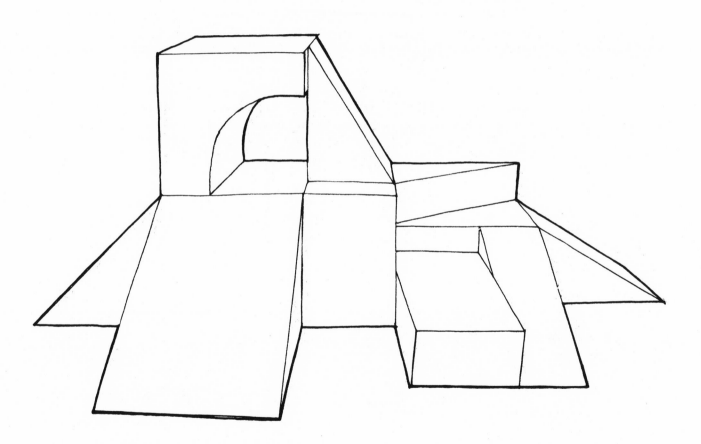

Unstructured playing with the blocks is critically important to the child's process of self-discovery and understanding. By conforming to fundamental relationships in Nature and many man-made objects, the Golden Mean Block system will provide the child with fundamental insights into many relationships between form and design. At the same time, the proportions inherent in the blocks will lend themselves to the reconstruction of those buildings made from the blocks based upon historical examples. Thus the child may be more readily able to comprehend the esthetic principles underlying both historic and contemporary design and architecture.

Traditionally, block construction and activities have been limited almost exclusively to the nursery school years. While the Golden Mean Block system is certainly intended for use by young children, we hope that the system will also be used at the middle and upper elementary levels.

THE COMPLETE BLOCK BOOK

was keyboarded on an Apple II Plus Microcomputer by the author,
interfaced with a Quadex 500/Compugraphic 8600
in 10-point Bookman and leaded 3 points with display in Microgramma
    Bold Extended by Emerald Graphic Systems;
printed on 50-pound, acid-free Warren Eggshell Cream paper stock,
Smythe-sewn and bound over binder's boards in Joanna Arrestox cloth,
also adhesive-bound with paper covers
by Maple-Vail Books Manufacturing Group, Inc.;
and published by
SYRACUSE UNIVERSITY PRESS
SYRACUSE, NEW YORK 13244-5160